The Success Makeover

A Xente Lifestyle

(Pronounced Zhin-Tā)

KEVIN JOHNSON

Cover design: Sebastian A. Ortiz, Red Liger Studios

ISBN: 978-1-4834-6486-2 (sc)
ISBN: 978-1-4834-6487-9 (e)

Library of Congress Control Number: 2017901227

Lulu Publishing Services rev. date: 2/22/2017

Contents

Xente:

Real People, Real Lives, Real Successes!

This book is dedicated in loving memory of

Francis (Mick) Nugent

Miguel Barron and Eric Johnson

Acknowledgments

I want to first thank **Maricela Johnson**, my incredible wife and love of my life, who patiently supported me throughout this entire journey. Patience is a virtue!

Next I want to give special thanks to two of the brightest individuals I've ever met: **Joseph Ambrose**, who encouraged me to put passion to print, and **Nick Falcetta**, who served as a critical sounding board as I developed the narrative for this book.

I also want to express my gratitude to **Dr. Denise Murmann** and **Michele Murmann** for agreeing to be the critical eye and voice of reason when reviewing the original manuscript.

Finally, I want to make one last plea to **you, the reader**. You intuitively know what truly matters in life. Don't wait for the right moment or the perfect opportunity to make a meaningful connection. The time is now. Success is not about what you accumulate in your life; it's about how well you pay attention to and connect to all aspects of your complete life.

Wisdom not to ignore: Do not listen to the words of people who like to hear themselves pontificate about things that don't really matter, for they fill you with vain hopes and dreams. They speak of dreams hoped for by their own desires or limitations; this has no divine substance or real fulfillment in life to speak of. (Based on Jeremiah 23:16)

1

Xente Preface
and Dare to Question

Preface: A Xente Lifestyle

The Xente lifestyle is a shift by everyday people to connect, activate, and reconnect (CARE) with their whole lives. Xente is the recapturing of what truly matters right now through a balanced approach to living. Xente is stimulated by the realization that while we all have ambitions for greater accomplishments, success doesn't have to be some uncertain, illusory point in the future or an achievement displayed by the rich or famous alone.

The Xente lifestyle helps you to recognize that true success is already an inherent part of your everyday life. Xente is about everyone, regardless of a person's status or abilities in life. The Xente live with the highest integrity, selflessly seeking to connect to the people and societal elements around them, making their world a more significant place as they fully engage it.

The Xente lifestyle promotes an intentional effort to take control of your existence through shifting your thinking about the chase for traditional success and expanding it to emphasize other important areas of your whole life. Doing so will create success that's achievable by all people and not exclusive to just a few, as is the case with traditional success.

We have the power to make a difference in our lives right now by connecting to the essential areas that are critical to a highly successful existence: family, friends, significant others, community, vocation, and self.

For the readers of this book who choose to follow the principles in part or whole, your lives will be transformed, and you will begin to create the kind of existence that will allow you to experience deeper relationships that include excitement, intimacy, spontaneity, joy, trust, integrity, belonging, security, faithfulness, connectedness, achievement, and balance, ultimately enabling you to experience a more fulfilled life.

Dare to question your current existence. Do you ever take the time to really dissect your life, asking these questions?

- Am I getting the most out of life?
- Am I truly connecting and relating to the many important lives around me?
- Am I unconsciously going through life wanting more but not necessarily understanding what "more" is—or how to get there?
- Why does happiness seem to be out of reach for me? Why is life so hard?

Please note that I did not highlight money because we all have a heightened focus on it. Do you find that even when you obtain more of it, it only provides temporary satisfaction, leaving you craving for—yes, you guessed it—more?

All of these questions may seem a bit philosophical in nature, but I would wager any amount of money that many of you know or have known someone who has pondered these very questions. Now, before you begin to reflect on these questions too deeply, I want to give you an opportunity to step outside of yourself. Be open to experiencing and relating to what could turn out to be more of a pivotal moment than you could ever imagine. I want to make the case that this pursuit of we call *more* is nothing less than our misaligned attempts to find or capture traditional success.

I'm sympathetic to the fact that most of us have a difficult time critically looking at our own lives to see the issues and opportunities that are so obvious to others. I want to provide a bird's-eye view of a common trek in life, allowing you to unearth for yourselves the impact caused by the chase for traditional success ("more"). This view will bear out one conclusion: our chase for success has set many of us up to be prime candidates for a present or eventual success makeover.

To help connect the dots, I want to bring us all to the same understanding and place us on even ground by imparting valuable context from which to establish the roots and premise behind Xente. Here it is:

> Xente is about everyone, regardless of a
> person's abilities or status in life.

2

Xente Definition and Premise

The origin of Xente (pronounced Hen-Tā): Xente is a Galician/Portuguese phrase meaning "real people." For the writings of this book, there was a need to create a new expression to define the lifestyle concepts presented. The new expression will encapsulate the urban definition associated with the Asian concept known as Zen (ultimately representing balance and harmony). Together, this newly adapted expression and articulation will be referred to as **Xente (pronounced Zhin-Tā).** This new expression will explicitly empower this book with truth to help illuminate a better way of living for our ever-evolving society.

To help bring the meaning of **Xente (Zhin-Tā)** to life, the new definition reads, "To purposefully interact or bond with the essential areas of one's complete life (i.e., family, friends, significant others, community, vocation, and self), producing greater significance, balance, and/or harmony. Or the act of creating success by connecting to what really matters in life."

The primary premise behind Xente was born out of an idea that you do not have to achieve traditional success in order to experience happiness, fulfillment, or significance. In fact, if we look closely, we will find that many of the very things in life designed to bring us happiness or the feeling of fulfillment are often right in front of us. The reason we typically don't consider the merits of this seemingly obvious point is because we've been trained by means of generational assimilation to believe that success is all about what you earn, where you live, or where you sit in society. In other words, because we have observed this way of living from our parents and they from their parents, we have adopted this typical definition of success as an empirical norm.

The concepts in this book will help you to reprogram those empirical norms, allowing you to see the often-neglected opportunities that have been right in front of you all along. In fact, once you review these simple yet effective concepts along with the relatable life examples, you may feel compelled to take an honest look at your life. In doing so, you will face one of two options: either you will make a conscious decision to ignore your current opportunities to live a complete life and continue down the path of chasing your tail to an uncertain end, or by being more intentional, you will begin to make simple yet impactful changes in the way you connect with your complete life to experience relationships and life anew.

I insist that if you intentionally introduce the concepts of this book into your life, you will not only find the happiness your heart longs for, but you will also find that you are more effective in every area of your life, whether personal or professional.

In order to help further validate the premise behind this concept, I want to draw your attention to what traditional success mainly represents today. Not leaving anything off the table, we will also expose the understated consequences that have been tolerated by those who wait (sometimes in agony) for their loved ones to finally reach their moment of actualization. The sad reality is that many never make it to the degree originally envisioned, as you will soon uncover or may already know.

> If we look closely, we will find that many of the very things in life designed to bring us happiness or the feeling of fulfillment are often right in front of us.

3

Traditional Success: The Real Story

Traditional success is by far the most sought-after endeavor, passed on to almost every man, woman, and child in existence. No matter what race, creed, or cultural background you represent, success will always be front and center for almost everyone who has greater personal aspirations or who simply wants to surpass the accomplishments previously earned by their generational counterparts (mom, dad, sister, brother, etc.).

Interestingly enough, our lackluster experience associated with harnessing traditional success hardly ever produces the kind of success often gazed upon, which leaves most of us in a constant state of wanting more or being unfulfilled.

This outcome is like going to your local thirty-one-flavor ice-cream parlor, in search of the one flavor they never seem to have, and walking out each time without exploring any of the other thirty flavors because you have convinced yourself there is only one flavor that really matters.

I am not sure about you, but this approach to taste-bud bliss seems like a ludicrous pattern, given that there are many other possibilities at your fingertips that could more than likely bring the desired joy you might be seeking. With many of us living our lives in a similar fashion, a great number of men and a rapidly growing number of women have literally given their entire lives without ever seeing their ultimate dream attained. To add insult to injury, many have sacrificed so much in their lives (e.g., time with family, meaningful relationships, their own health, peace of mind, etc.) to achieve that one flavor of success that in so many ways positions us to be the dog chasing its own tail—a never-ending journey.

According to Merriam-Webster's online dictionary, the definition of success is "the fact of getting or achieving wealth, respect, or fame." This absolutely makes sense and is clearly part of the reason for so much attention by the masses. However, Merriam-Webster's dictionary also offers an alternate definition: "the correct or desired result of an attempt" (http://www.merriam-webster.com/dictionary/success).

While success in itself indicates the achievement of wealth, respect, and/or fame, it clearly offers a broader alternative that has greater applications far beyond our traditional thinking. Understanding the important distinction between the two—particularly what it could create in one's life when chosen properly—you may feel compelled to change your traditional thinking with regard to success. This will alleviate the narrow outcomes associated with our narrow views.

It will also allow the expanded definition of success to take priority in the fore thinking of our minds, to illuminate the many possibilities rarely focused on because we are too busy chasing the mainstream media's idea of success. Keeping this in mind, let's take an even closer look at the alternate definition, to provide some practical examples to help bring home the points expressed.

Again, the alternate definition of success reads: "the correct or desired result of an attempt." What this definition is pointing out is that no matter what you set your sights on in life, as long as you achieve what's desired, you can count it as success. For the purposes of this book, I am also going to add what's appropriate (keeping in mind that not all things one might desire are appropriate). The beauty of this definition is that it is not trying to point you in any direction per se; it is merely suggesting that anything you deem worth placing your individual focus around could represent a success goal. *This is the key distinction that sets the concepts of Xente apart from the traditional definition connected to success.*

Taking this idea a step further allows me to share the following examples.

Example 1: An individual may decide to spend thirty minutes exercising each day, to establish a better pattern of health. As this individual is making a positive impact against his or her personal goal, he or she can count this as success as long as the effort is being applied and met in some way. Even if the individual spends thirty minutes every other day (versus each day), this intentional attempt against this goal will create a pattern of success that will likely grow over time.

Example 2: A father has determined that he has allowed his extended hours in the office to take him away from his family for far too long. As a result, he has committed to spend more quality time with his family by setting up dedicated time twice per week, without any disruptions from work or home duties. As long as his attempts are completed according to his desired outcome, he can also count that as success.

For the remainder of this book, I will continue to focus on real-life scenarios that will highlight what I am calling the essential areas of life. (I will get to that in a moment.)

Now allow me to highlight the mainstream media's depiction of success, to demonstrate the counter position. This should help you make the ultimate choice between a Xente life and a life that follows the traditional success pattern. The mainstream media's description of success airs visions of prosperity, unlimited freedom, elevated status, increased power, and large bank accounts; giving those who dare to dream a glimpse of what life might be like, to "satisfy" all of their natural and sometimes unnatural desires.

The undeniable appetite for success has been the driving force that has, without a doubt, allowed mankind to produce some of the greatest developments this world has ever seen. There is no doubt that success has long created the allure or prospect of freedom or security, and for those who have managed to accomplish this elusive endeavor, I am certain many of the outcomes often gazed upon hold true.

However, we are often captivated by only *part* of the story. Success—or the chase for it—has singlehandedly been the biggest excuse for ignoring the other areas of our lives that bring the greatest fulfillment one can experience. Did you ever notice the overwhelming response when someone is asked about the things that most make them happy? It's typically unrelated to money or acquiring material possessions. In fact, the answer runs much deeper than these superficial aspirations. The real answer is, and always has involved, our natural instinct to personally connect with what matters the most.

It's been said that the best things in life are often free, and the primary focus around this concept has always centered around our family, friends, loved ones, and the life causes that pull on our heartstrings. When polled about this subject (putting work aside for just a moment), most people would tell you that these areas by far are the most important aspects of their lives.

Interestingly enough, if you polled the same people, they would genuinely argue that the principal way to experience happiness within these areas would come through them making a run at or achieving traditional success—as if that single success factor would somehow be the magic potion needed to engage the life around them.

Frankly, it's this type of thinking that's ultimately responsible for preventing us from experiencing success more holistically. This traditional approach to life has been such an understated or otherwise marginalized concept that when confronted with its obvious consequences, we tend to shrug it off. We have accepted that chasing after traditional success has become a "normal" way of life, or it's the price you have to pay to enjoy the ultimate benefits of life.

This is simply not true; it does not have to be that way. In reality, if you have the audacity to step outside of your comfort zone and challenge the illogical thinking that essentially says you have to be unhappy now to eventually be happy one day, then keep reading. This book will change your life.

If you haven't guessed by now, this book is not about how you obtain wealth or how you go about crafting your ultimate career. Neither is it about how following the routines of others can make you successful.

This book underscores our absolute need to recognize and change our narrow view of success and to bring into focus an expanded view, to allow us to find joy and satisfaction in our lives right now, versus some unknown point in the future.

I know what's going through your head at this point: the idea of you experiencing a successful life right now appears to be idealistic or out of reach, based on your assimilated ideas. But what if I told you that achieving success was only a matter of modifying how you viewed and connected with what was already right in front of you? What if I told you that most of us have been delaying our own happiness because our perception of what success has been has created a blind spot? What if I told you we are trapped by our own ambitions, and the sooner we discover it, the sooner we can begin to piece our lives together? This would allow us to not only appreciate all the essential areas we often put aside but also allow us to finally take a deep breath and encounter real success with the real lives we have today.

Fellow success seekers, I am a simple, ordinary person. I live a fairly common life with common life issues, with hopes and dreams just like the next person, but I have to believe that the experiences I am going to share are not germane to me alone. In fact, I am betting that no matter what walk of life you come from, my story is probably more common than not.

The reason for referencing my own personal story is not a ploy to draw out the dramatic but a way to paint a vivid picture that will allow you to spot the pitfalls that sidetrack our happiness. This is the very place at which all of our stories connect. You may be asking yourself, what's the significance of our stories connecting? My hope is that, like me, you will also begin to realize the many real successes that are already evident in your life as you currently live it. Or that you will begin to visualize the possibilities connected with furthering your personal success journey—not as some far-off mirage, but as a viable reality that's achievable regularly through your own intentional acts of connecting and interacting with who and what matters the most.

No one is an island unto him- or herself, so I want to warn you in advance that my story is so common, you may not immediately see the hook that continues to snag so many of us. In fact, you may see so many similarities that you may be tempted to view or justify them as common everyday occurrences. I caution you from allowing this to happen.

As I take you through my brief story, you will begin to see how innocent and humble the chase starts out and how it eventually takes on a life of its own. If your story is anything like mine—and there is a great possibility that it is—you might begin staring back into time, wondering where it all went or asking yourself, *How did I get here?*

Worse, you may start wishing you could go back in time to change something that happened or didn't happen.

For me, the realization that my story and time had taken on a life of its own included a harsh reality check. It was the reality that ended with me writing this book. I hope to provide a warning and easily attainable solutions, so others might stop the madness. This madness is driving so many of us further and further away from the very things that could bring us the happiness and fulfillment our lives and the people around us desire.

> "A great number of men and a rapidly growing number of women have literally given their entire lives without ever seeing their ultimate dream attained."

4

The Perpetual Day in the Life

Does your day resemble this at all? I wake up wanting more time on the clock to simply rest and recapture some of the life that seems to unconsciously pass me by. But with the shadow of responsibility lurking over me and the strength propelled by my ambition, I give the clock another stare, convincing myself that it's only 4:00 a.m. The exhaustion I am feeling will pass, and I will soon be pedaling the time away on the elliptical machine. I know that getting up and exercising at this hour of the morning makes as much sense to me as banging my head against a brick wall.

However, working past this feeling, I know that the early-morning rise is, in reality, fueled by my motivation to get into the office ahead of my peers. That way, I can maintain the pace of "success" that allows me to preserve the good reputation and advantage that's been so hard to come by. Oddly enough, I keep telling myself that my early-morning rise was a way to build in quality time to spend with my family at the end of a hard day, versus spending it in a sweaty gym.

The truth of the matter is that my perceived act of valor wasn't all about an overwhelming desire to spend more time with my family (at least not primarily). In fact, it became another excuse I used to further my ambitions for "success." This would eventually push me further away from making meaningful connections with my family and other critical areas of my life. As a result, this long and exhausting routine continued to be the cadence of my life, all in the name of success. On the surface, this may not seem like a big deal, but I think most of us find ourselves captive to a similar pattern in some way, shape, or form.

However, when studied carefully, this pattern highlights a pace of life that exposes the truth about what has become our greatest obsession. This obsession has resulted in a life filled with superficial connections with loved ones and friends, perpetuating a stress-filled life of perceived shortcomings. The name of this obsession is the pursuit of traditional success.

5

My Story

I grew up in the inner city, raised by my grandmother. The environment in the home was filled with love and plenty of discipline. However, outside of the home, our neighborhood was inundated with illegal activity, consisting of violence, gangs, and drugs. My family did everything they could to expose my brother and me to the best environment possible, so they sent us to private schools. This was great because we received a quality education. But even with that, we still lived in a neighborhood where crime ruled the streets. As a result, I was often exposed to dangerous or questionable situations.

In spite of the environment where I was raised, I was able to finish grade school and high school with minimal complications or physical harm. After high school, I went to a local junior college. Schoolwork was the furthest thing from my mind. I can say this because the main reason I attended a local college was to nurture the relationship with my high school sweetheart. We were so attached at that point that we couldn't imagine being separated for any amount of time. However, shortly after my first year in college, we found ourselves in a life-changing situation—I learned I was going to be a father. As you can imagine, the stress of that forthcoming responsibility overwhelmed my girlfriend and me.

This was the start of my innocent and premature entrance into the rat race called life. Having no real experiences to help us, my soon-to-be wife and I struggled for a number of years. I started taking jobs that utilized my physical abilities, as I had no other abilities to fall back on. There was nothing I wasn't willing to do to take care of my family.

I worked in a restaurant as a pizza maker, I worked for a ceramic tile installation company as a laborer, and I cleaned and waxed commercial floors at night. I also worked for a small telemarketing agency, and I even started my own cleaning business, where I cleaned people's homes. This honest physical work lasted long enough for me to realize that this was not what my dreams were supposed to be. In spite of these experiences, I still had an incredible hope that I was meant to do something special with my life; this included having dreams of a great job, big house, fancy car, and enough money to do whatever my heart desired. (How naive and idealistic was I?)

Nevertheless, my naiveté allowed my thinking to be the driving force behind everything I did from that point forward. After struggling in those labor-intensive jobs for a number of years, I finally received an opportunity in sales at a small firm that offered computer-wire and customized-cable assemblies. I discovered I had a natural affinity for business. This led me to a series of opportunities that allowed me to not only learn about sales and business operations but gave me the chance to expand my skills enough to make some significant contributions. In fact, I continued on a path of making the most of every career decision I made from that point forward. I took on the jobs no one else wanted, believing that my attitude would eventually advance me.

My mantra summed up my attitude: "Even if you are on the right track, if you just sit there, you will eventually be run over." During this period of my career, I was at the peak of my motivation, especially for anything that had to do with career advancement or earning more money. My focus was so intense that I not only put in long hours in the office, but when I arrived home in the evening, I would put in another two to four hours and not even bat an eye. I was very proud of the reputation I built for myself by always being the first one in the office and the last one to sign off at the end of every night.

The guiding principle for my career was vested in the idea that if I worked harder than everyone else, management would have to notice and reward my efforts. For the most part, I was spot-on in the strategy that I set for myself—up to that point. As the momentum of life began to rapidly build in pace, I began to seize additional career opportunities. Some were presented to me because of my positive results and great work ethic, and others I asked for based on the respect I had earned from my superiors and my peers.

The interesting predicament occurring the whole time was that my satisfaction associated with these achievements only lasted long enough for me to plot out my next move. Don't get me wrong—I spent valuable time working the opportunities that were presented to me, but I was never truly satisfied because I knew there was more out there for me. The troubling fact was that if you asked me, I really could not articulate what the *more* was. I just knew it was out there and that I wanted whatever it was.

As a result, this quest for advancement and wanting more success continued to be a perpetual cycle of dissatisfaction, as the challenges of life around me began to outweigh my short-lived accomplishments. Because of this recurring pattern, I was not experiencing the joy of traditional success—so much so that I began to examine this cycle that continued to entangle me. I concluded that I was chasing the kind of success that may not be attainable for two reasons. First, I more than likely couldn't attain that type of success because I had not learned to embrace the traditional success I already achieved; and second, because the other aspects of my life were so out of sync, I would not have enough support to enjoy "success," even if I finally did achieve it.

Truth be told, there wasn't one area of my life that wasn't negatively impacted by my chase. In fact, you probably won't be surprised to hear that by this point in my life, my marriage was basically hanging on by a frayed string.

There was no doubt that I loved my high school sweetheart of almost fifteen years by this time. But because we were often like two ships passing in the night, connecting on any level—emotionally, physically, intellectually or socially— was a scheduling nightmare because of the priorities I had set for myself. For the occasions where there was time, I was so exhausted I could hardly pay attention.

About the same time, another casualty was the negative impact my success chase had on my children, who simply desired more time and nurturing from me as they were growing up. It's eye-opening to experience firsthand how the loss of quality time with your children can morph into a different set of problems that impacts them not only as children but eventually as adults. In fact, I recall one sobering moment my wife once brought to my attention. My youngest daughter, a preteen at the time, mentioned that she envied her best friend because she had an incredible relationship with her father. She often observed her friend and father embracing or giving each other a kiss or simply saying they loved one another.

My daughter went on to tell her mom that she didn't think I loved her because I never did any of those things with her or her sister. Then she asked my wife why I couldn't love her the way her friend's father loved his daughter. Of course, my wife did what any good mother would do and assured her that I did love her. She told our daughter that she needed to try to understand that because I loved them so much, that was the main reason I worked so hard and did my best to provide for their needs.

The fact was, I did love my daughters with a deep passion, but I had never experienced my own true example of how to display those sentiments in a way that would clearly express the feelings that were genuinely inside of me. I learned to believe that when you love your children, you work hard and provide for their needs, no matter what it takes. (This was definitely a concept I assimilated into my life very well.) Besides, I believed that I had turned out okay, given my childhood experience with the hard-work-equals-love concept.

In my family, none of us shared our love in a physical way through hugs or kisses or by verbal means like saying "I love you." I openly accepted the fact that most of the material needs provided to me modeled the kind of love I was okay with. Admittedly, I had no real clue about the way not displaying love tangibly would impact me, let alone others. It's a fact I am painfully aware of today as I observe my daughter's approach to her own life.

While my daughter is beautiful and smart, she often comes across as an unsure little girl looking for love in all the wrong places. Concealed by my responsibility for taking care of the family, I now realize that my hyper-focused quest for traditional success hindered me from connecting with her in a way that would have made a difference in her life then, today, and perhaps for the rest of her life. Because of my lack of consistent effort to offer time and attention with her, she's paying the price with a multitude of concerns that include issues with authority, intimacy, acceptance, self-worth and who knows what else. How do you make up for that kind of impact?

Unfortunately, the story doesn't get any better as I provide a further glimpse into other areas of my life. During that same period of time, I also discovered my commitment to serve in my community took a similar direction to my job. I always had a heart for giving back to the community, through my church, musical talents, or serving with an organization that helped the blind and hearing impaired.

Much like at my job, I habitually did exactly what I said I would do. This sounds good, right? But this was another impact of the traditional, success-driven life I was leading. It included not having the ability to say no to anything asked of me (professionally, that is). Living a life with very few boundaries, if I could figure out a way to squeeze it into my schedule, I would go for it. You better believe that if said I was going to do it, then it was as good as done. Imagine with me for a moment what it took to maintain my full-time work schedule, serve as the church treasurer, keep musical obligations, teach Bible classes, and sell real estate—all at the same time. This is by no means an exaggeration of the schedule I kept.

Talk about stress! All of this resulted in me working myself into such a condition that I couldn't even begin to tell you what I wanted in any part of my life. This was mainly because I lost valuable perspective for what was actually occurring. I had left a trail of nothing but superficial accomplishments. Even though I had totally lost my balance, I still had the ability to do what I trained myself to do: continue to perform and take advantage of the work-related opportunities given to me. This was all great if I was looking to conquer the world without regard to the broken relationships produced by my seemingly innocent intentions. Well, as the saying goes, too much of anything is a bad thing; trust me, I was up to my chin in it.

With the exhaustion of a mother caring for newborn twins, I continued this pace until I was unable to function properly, succumbing to physical ailments that eventually shut me down. It started out as a cold; then it turned into a month long sinus infection, but I did not let that stop me because I had commitments I needed to keep. Shortly after the sinus infection began to subside, I was still having issues because my physical energy never returned. In fact, I began getting massive migraine headaches, and my vision became very blurry. My body was going through continual hot and cold flashes. Then I had the constant need to visit the restroom what seemed like every hour on the hour.

After enduring these symptoms for a few weeks, I began to experience cotton mouth and was unable to keep anything down. Surprisingly enough, through this period of time, I still continued to keep up my pace of life until one morning I literally could not get out of bed. I had to ask my wife to help me up so I could finally go to the emergency room. That day, the attending doctors revealed a diagnosis of type-2 diabetes (which clearly resulted from the nearly 320 pounds I had amassed from poor diet, lack of sleep, and little to no exercise that existed well before my early-morning rise).

This ailment did not begin at birth. It began because my pace of life had caught up with me. I had finally started to experience the true effects of what the unmeasured chase for traditional success could do to an individual who did not consider all aspects that make up a valued existence.

For whatever reason, when you are obsessed with the chase, you never picture anything like this happening to you. Looking back, at that point there was no doubt the outcome of that lifestyle was totally self-inflicted. Sadly enough, I had all of the warning signs along the way with firsthand experiences, but I continued to ignore them because I made the traditional success chase the most important aspect of my life. It's ironic that when life comes crashing down, you briefly find time to take a deep breath and see the blessings that have already occurred in your life. But it's just as ironic how you quickly jump right back into your old routines as if nothing ever occurred.

> "This quest for advancement and wanting more success continued to be a perpetual cycle of dissatisfaction as the challenges of life around me began to outweigh my short-lived accomplishments."

6

Hard Knocks of Reality

Friends, I am no different than you; it's just that I've had plenty of unsolicited incidents or circumstances driving me to take another hard look at the choices I had been making over the course of my narrowly focused life. I must admit to you that I did not suddenly have a revelation, even after all I had experienced up to that point. It actually took another series of trials and a tragic event before my "success veil" began to rip right before my very eyes.

In fact, my life-changing revelation didn't come until one particular event that made me look in the mirror and ask: "What am I chasing, and why am I chasing it so hard?"

This self-reflection came after what I considered the most tragic of all such events: the death of my close friend Mick.

By coincidence, Mick was the person who handled all of my financial and life-planning events. I recall that every time I used to travel or go away on business trips, I got in the habit of reminding my wife to call Mick if anything were to happen to me; he would know exactly what to do. All those years, I intuitively felt that my lifespan would be shorter than his. I vividly remember that day and the phone call from Mick's wife that forever changed my perspective about the chase for traditional success. Initially I thought it was a bit strange that she would be calling me. Then she told me the news: Mick had a massive heart attack the night before and had died. I was stunned. I had no words of comfort—or any words, for that matter; there was no logical response for this bombshell that overwhelmed me. In fact, all I could gather myself to say at that moment was "Oh no." This tragic event caused me to evaluate the things with which I had been occupying my time.

What if it had been me who died instead of Mick? What regrets would I have? Trust me when I tell you, I thought of too many regrets to count and so many opportunities with loved ones missed.

As you can imagine, the difficulty of losing Mick was disturbing on many levels, especially because he was survived by his wife and four young children. The oldest was soon to be eleven years old, and the youngest was barely four. (Not to mention the fact that I had been so preoccupied with chasing my own set of dreams all in the name of traditional success.)

Thinking back, the conversations I had with friends and loved ones following that event only made me feel emptier, mainly because I knew how hard Mick had worked. I specifically remembered our conversations about how much he desired to see the results of his hard work and what it could bring to his growing family. His premature death was not the story any of us would have ever imagined—not for him or for any of us, for that matter. I know some of you have experienced and can share very similar stories that have touched your own lives.

Mick's death made me realize that it really didn't matter so much anymore that I was tracking well toward my traditional success goals or that I had been giving it my all and had achieved a few meaningless things. In fact, none of those things were relevant at all when compared to the loss of someone's life. Experiencing this painful reality as my new truth, I want to dispel the myth that if you can get that incredible job—making a lot of money or achieving your dream of acquiring fame or fortune ("traditional success")—everything will fall into place. That is total nonsense, and we have all been led down a rosy path full of thorns.

The most important thing I learned from Mick's death was that our relationships and time with family and friends are what matter the most. Our work is important, and we need to give it just attention, but it cannot fill the void of a loved one on any level, whether they are gone or still here with us. In fact, learning to accept our jobs or vocations as the smaller priority (or equal at best) when aligned against our lives and other essential areas is the most important aspect of living.

If you don't think so, just look at the lives of some "famous" people who have passed on or even those who may still be living. On the surface, they appear to have it all, not wanting for any material thing but are obviously desperately searching for something to fill the void that afflicts their lives. Failing to reach true happiness in the midst of their highly envied success, in one way or another, they are unceremoniously put on display for the entire world to see. This reveals their drug use/overdosing, broken relationships, public nuisance, depression, violence, financial ruin or financial deception (and the list goes on). Surely our drive for traditional success could not be leading us in a similar direction, could it?

Observing these common life situations repeated time and time again, I know I am not the only one who witnesses or feels the impact of this daily struggle. I am convinced even more than ever that we have to redefine our traditional view or fixation with success. To do this we must relearn our concept of success—not to enable a world of mediocrity but to reset our expectations to emphasize the life we have now, basically accepting the success that exists as we live an honest, productive, everyday life.

Following the lifestyle approaches in this book will help us shed the silent guilt we unconsciously (and sometimes consciously) harbor deep inside. The impact of this approach will allow each of us to grasp and experience all opportunities for real engagement, whether we are speaking of traditional success or the areas of life that we profess as the things that matter most (e.g., family, relationships, health, commitment, etc.).

Are you beginning to see how these life conditions might have a connection to that of your own or perhaps to someone close to you? These are real situations, experienced by real people who are making real-life attempts at a happier, more fulfilling life, despite the feelings or challenges they face each day. These stories and conditions of life are truly about you and me. Just take a look around you—we are not alone.

I can see it all over the faces of people everywhere I go. In fact, I have been commuting to work for years and can share that the one thing I observe most frequently is exhausted people fighting their way through this life. People are so preoccupied with their own journey that they have a hard time even looking at others with a simple smile, let alone extending common courtesy.

I once witnessed a woman fall in the middle of a busy metropolitan street and was shocked to see more than a half dozen people simply step over and around her, not even offering one helping hand. What's wrong with that picture? We are in such a hurry to get nowhere fast that we do not even realize how quickly life is passing us by. This seems to be a common issue plaguing most of western society, and it is on the rise in other emerging nations as they view the United States as a model for success.

> "We must relearn our concept of success, not to enable a world of mediocrity but to reset our expectations to emphasize the life we have now, accepting the success that exists as we live an honest, productive, everyday life."

7

Success Unveiled

I'm not taking anything away from what we in the United States have accomplished. In fact, we have pushed the level of success to an art form by capitalizing on industry and yielding the most out of everyday people like you and me. At the same time, we have managed to tear down the necessary fabric of our personal lives, leaving it riddled with unintentional sacrifice and missed moments, in order to harness everything traditional success has to offer.

This issue has become somewhat of a mockery by us as we view other countries as compared to our nation. Haven't you ever heard friends or family who visit other parts of the world share how laid back or slow life is? It's almost as if we see that as a problem.

I've got news for you: our neighboring countries are not the ones living with extreme success-induced problems—we are. It is our way of life that drives some of us to early graves, broken relationships, and constant feelings of dissatisfaction.

It's a fact that our employers call for us to perform on our jobs and continually strive to exceed the goals established; after all, that's what we get paid to do. Instead we have become a society of individuals emboldened by entitlement, which feeds into our very nature to desire more. As a byproduct, we have innocently raised our children with even greater appetites through generational assimilation. This includes nurturing a hyper obsession for the very thing that either may not be in our immediate reach or takes nearly a lifetime to achieve.

The interesting paradox is that we have seen a fair number of people achieve the dream of traditional success and find they are just as distraught in many areas of their lives as the rest of us. You heard me; we are all in the same boat, success or no success. Could there be more to success than what we have learned throughout our waking lives?

I know I am laying it on heavy, and this may be hard for some of you to accept. I get it; I certainly would not have accepted this truth so readily, especially because I have been obsessed with my own chase. Let me offer this as food for thought: one study showed that the top 1 percent of our nation's wealthiest people holds as much wealth as the bottom 90 percent. In fact, an article on guardian.com (published November 13, 2014) stated: "Not since the great depression has wealth inequality in the US been so acute" (http://www.theguardian.com/business/2014/nov/13/us-wealth-inequality-top-01-worth-as-much-as-the-bottom-90).

If this statement is true, then at what point do we embrace our own level of success and start living the life that is before us?

If we take a simple look around us, we'll see that a great number of us are primed for an intervention.

It has become obvious that our quest for prosperity has only led us to an overstressed society of scarcely engaged individuals who are waiting for someone or something to release the pressure valve.

As a byproduct of our chase, we have accumulated so much debt trying to garner a taste of what success feels like that we can't see our way through the cloud of debt lingering over us, let alone the added stress this creates. Is this really what the hunt for traditional success is all about?

Consider for a moment the impact of this stress-filled way of life. Research has shown that stress can have many physical and mental side effects on our bodies over prolonged periods.

In fact, an article published on Psychcentral.com lists what may be some very familiar side effects of stress. Are any of these familiar to you?

- Insomnia
- Increased heart rate
- General restlessness
- Nervousness
- High blood pressure
- Fatigue
- Constant worry
- Forgetfulness
- A sense of being overwhelmed/overworked
- Poor work relations

Keep in mind this list is by no means an exhaustive representation of issues (http://psychcentral.com/lib/the-impact-of-stress/).

How did so many of us get to this place? It did not happen overnight; for most of us, it more than likely developed over an extended period of time, slowly and unassumingly edging its way into every crevice of our lives.

It's amazing that you never see it coming because it typically starts out under very ordinary circumstances. Before you know it, you are blindsided by life and the quest for traditional success as the prescription to address all of life's concerns.

> "It has become so obvious that our quest for prosperity has only led us to an overstressed society of scarcely engaged individuals who are waiting for someone or something to release the pressure valve."

8

The Prominent
1–2 Percent

Who really achieves this elusive "traditional success"? Somewhere along life's way, I acquired the thought that everyone had the right to create success. I believe most of us were indoctrinated with the same notion. However, the reality is that most people spend an entire lifetime chasing traditional success, only to find they've exhausted much of their lives chasing the one kind of success that traditionally has been achieved by a very small percentage of our nation's population. This is not a random overstatement.

In fact, according to research data developed by the federal congressional budget office, in 2007 the richest 1 percent of the American population possessed 34.6 percent of the country's total wealth, and the next 19 percent of the population held 50.5 percent. This means that the top 20 percent of Americans controlled 85 percent of the country's wealth, and the remaining 80 percent of the population shared in the remaining 15 percent.

Adding insult to injury, after the great recession, which started in 2007, the total share of wealth held by the top 1 percent of the population actually grew from 34.6 percent to 37.1 percent, and the amount controlled by the top 20 percent of Americans grew from 85 percent to 87.7 percent.

During that same period of time, the median household wealth also dropped by 36.1 percent compared to 11.1 percent for the top 1 percent, creating a bigger gap between the 1 percent and the 99 percent of everyday people. Just to put these data points into perspective, if you consider all the people you will ever know or meet in your lifetime, only one or two out of every hundred individuals or families may experience some form of wealth or traditional success, as compared to the remaining population of individuals you encounter.

Put yet another way, the majority of people you know or will meet will have to survive life with very humble to moderate means (relative to traditional success). This is important to know and understand because the one thing that consumes a great many of us is the one thing most of us may never have the ability to attain statistically—or at least not at the level many of us dream of or strive for each day.

Some of you may find this to be extremely disturbing or even consider this to be hot air. Even if this particular set of facts doesn't apply to you, the opportunity to broaden and balance your view of success can allow you to experience life in a more complete manner. For those of you who have come to a similar revelation regarding the concepts outlined in this book, your awareness and deliberate actions will allow you to see the many existing and new possibilities that will offer an expanded view of success versus the one-dimensional view that has been the preoccupation of our hearts and minds.

I want to direct you to what I failed to catch sight of for many years. The thing I was looking for had mostly been right in front of me all along, and all it took was for me to acknowledge my reality and pay attention to what was surrounding me. When I did, here is what I learned: success was already an inherent part of my daily life, but I did not recognize it because I was gauging everything through my traditional success-colored lenses. Ironically enough, this view applies to most of us, whether we are part of the 1 percent or the 99 percent.

I want to make it clear that the lifestyle approach expressed in this book isn't a departure from any of your hopes and dreams. In fact, I will argue that if we were more effectively living a complete, balanced life, utilizing all of the gifts and talents we possess, it may accelerate or heighten our chances for levels of "traditional" success. Who knows, one could even wind up being in the rare 1 to 2 percent of the population (and have the benefits of holistic success, Xente). However, for those of you who have been feeling the overwhelming stress borne by the chase for traditional success without a clear or reasonable way of achieving it in sight, stop. Now is your chance to reflect briefly on what it is you are chasing. Ask yourself, what do you really want out of life? What would make you feel more fulfilled or happy?

Did your answers include more money? A bigger house? Another car? A better job? Or maybe greater status? For some of us, maybe this quest for traditional success is bleeding over into our personal desires of wanting a "different" or "better" partner in life. Come on! Stop it with the narrow thinking, and don't be deceived by your own desire for more things that really don't matter in the real scheme of life.

What's interesting about our personal relationships (significant others) is that we typically reflect on scenarios that superficially make us feel good.

However, to the detriment of so many of us, we have a harder time seeing the pitfalls or traps that eventually come crashing down around us. Again, I am not pointing fingers at anyone; this is a reality I have observed time and time again. I am wagering that most of you have seen similar scenarios as well.

What's the point to this self-actualized rant? It's simple: we miss out on the best things in life because we simply don't focus on our complete life. I am talking about the real successes that can and are already happening all around us, but they are hard to see, simply because we keep hanging on to the world's narrow view of success (traditional success).

> "Success was already an inherent part of my daily life, but I did not recognize it because I was gauging everything through my traditional success-colored lenses."

9

Real-Life Success

I know it's difficult to put aside our ingrained views about success, but no matter what walk of life you come from or how complex your current life is, you can experience real-life success today. In fact, as stated previously, success is already a part of our everyday existence; we simply do a poor job of giving ourselves credit for it. As the saying goes, Rome wasn't built in a day. Given this premise alone, every daily success or achievement we recognize and credit ourselves with is a small step toward a more significant one. In fact, without some pattern of daily success, there is no way you could ever achieve greater accomplishments. Ancient Roman engineering captured the essence of this idea.

Let's take the Rome expression a bit further and use something abstract like getting out of bed. Most of us take for granted the power of what this simple act does with respect to our lives. Here's the rundown.

- **Success 1.** In order for many of the incredible structures of Rome to eventually be built, surely the Roman builders needed to get out of bed; the structures couldn't be done while builders were snuggling up to their favorite pillow.
- **Success 2.** Getting out of bed once, twice, or every other day was not good enough. They needed to do this simple yet important act on a consistent basis.
- **Success 3.** As a consistent pattern of awakening was established, they also needed to show up to the job site ready, willing, and with the right attitude to work.
- **Success 4.** Once on the job, a common plan synchronized the efforts of all the Roman workers to get the common task of a single day or a structure completed (intentionality).
- **Success 5.** These consistent daily accomplishments made by the Roman builders created enormous success and gave birth to some of the greatest innovations this world has ever seen. In fact, the same Roman ingenuity still plays an important role

in our society and in engineering today. (This is generational success. Keep this in mind.)

You may be chuckling, given the example I used, but in all of my years of managing people in corporate America, this idea of getting out of bed, showing up every day, being ready and willing to work or make meaningful contributions is not as simple as it may seem. It takes commitment and intentionality applied against the normal everyday things in life to make a difference or impact. Make no mistakes about it: every time you focus on the seemingly little things, it makes a difference and creates tangible success to build upon.

I know this is a far cry from our normal everyday thinking. But this view will help you to keep perspective on the things that should matter.

To bring this idea a little closer to home, the following examples might remind you of some very typical scenarios you may not consider as real success in your own life—but they are.

- Raising a family
- Completing educational endeavors
- Maintaining your kids' busy schedules
- Volunteering at the local food pantry

- Making time for school events with children
- Helping your neighbor with a project
- Spending time with friends
- Spending time and caring for the aged in your life
- Maintaining good, team-building relationships at work
- Waking up each day and being a productive member of society
- Making time in your day to exercise
- Courting your significant other (you heard me)
- Starting new friendships
- Stepping out of your comfort zone for others' sake
- Taking the time to really listen to your children
- Being in the moment (if at home, be at home; if at work, be at work)
- Being an encourager to others around you
- Keeping regular connections with extended family (grandparents, aunts, uncles, etc.)
- Intentionally maintaining balance in every aspect of your life (including time for yourself)

I see real people making successful strides like this every day without taking any credit for what they've done for others or for what they've personally accomplished themselves along the way.

Reflecting on these examples, I now understand that we're not meant to be alone in this struggle. Yet we take on life as if it was meant to be that way. We are truly a network of people meant to connect and made to support one another. Without this kind of connectivity, life doesn't seem to have the level of balance, fulfillment, or meaning needed to make it truly sustainable.

Without real connectivity, our perspective about life becomes a series of happenings leading us nowhere but to the next situation in life.

I could have overlooked the embedded views about the obsession for success, claiming it was just the way of life and kept it moving. However, I chose to acknowledge that the mad cycle I had been going through, albeit self-induced, could only be corrected by my own proactive actions. I am not hammering this point home because I decided that writing this book would be good therapy for me. In fact, my observation of the world in action confirmed that I was not an exception to the rule, but rather another participant in this massively complex game called life.

It's been said that the personal recognition of a problem is half the battle to solving it, and I couldn't agree more. Keeping this in mind, we each have the opportunity to take a step back right now and reflect on our lives. Our perspective has mostly been about what we can get or acquire in life. However, in many cases, I have realized that giving (not necessarily money) makes a big difference in how I feel about my own life.

For example, making the most of my relationships, giving my time, sharing my talents and knowledge, or caring for others can make a huge difference. The problem is clearly not that we have dreams or want to be successful; the issue is that we have made life and success mostly about our dreams or the chase for traditional success. As a result, we have lived our lives woefully disjointed and out of balance. This would be like trying to run a marathon with a broken ankle.

Real success for real people is not all about a mere point in time where you can say you have "made it." (Remember, most people don't "make it," according to statistics). Real success is about the entire journey along the way to your dream or success. If a person gives up his or her essential life connections to attain traditional success and has no one to enjoy it with, would that kind of success be worth it? Contrary to popular perspective, a Xente type lifestyle keeps your dream in sight but also recognizes that success is the ability to embrace your complete life.

Taking a balanced, intentional approach is a way of reminding us that true success is yet another opportunity to be successful in every aspect of our lives, which includes relationships with significant others, family, friends, community, and yes, even our vocations.

Learn to savor your connections in life, and remember your real connections are not five hundred friends on social media. Your connections are the people and things that matter the most in your life. We have to get out of our rat-race mentality. A constant connection to the rat race creates an impatience with life in general, and some of our dissatisfaction in life comes when we have to wait, which makes us rush. Life and true success is an investment in time with what matters. We must ask ourselves, if time is so valuable, why are we always rushing? It's because we need success now (or should I say we want relief now). What if you could tap into that success today? Would it change your perspective on how you deal with your everyday life? Would it help you to be in the moment?

To further expand on this concept of balancing life and achieving real success, think about this: "A journey of a thousand miles begins with a single step" Life is huge! Stop trying to consume life or success as if it were your last meal. Enjoy the journey, take a look around you, see the roses, and yes, smell them. Real-life success becomes what and where we place our focus. Would you rather take the chance on your current life strategy, continuing to battle in this rat race for the vision of a day that may never come? Or would you like to experience joy and success daily, while still being hopeful that one day you will realize your ultimate success or dream? I am not sure about you, but more frequent (or daily) success now sounds like a better option, simply because there is no promise of tomorrow for any of us.

> "Every daily success or achievement we recognize and credit ourselves with is a small step toward a more significant one.".

10

Fighting the Good Fight

Reflect for a moment: if any part of these truths associated with the chase resembles your thinking or walk of life, you can't help but wonder what will be the catalyst to bring your life back into 20/20 focus. What's it going to take for you to recognize the best of who you are or who you could be, to embrace what matters the most around you, in order to help you enjoy success right where you are today? To do this effectively, you must be able to self-evaluate and test your *perceived* reality with others, in order to see what you have become and more importantly what you have been missing or perhaps neglecting.

Then you must actively reengage every essential area of your life to restore it to the way it should have been all along. It's through the intentional engagement of your essential areas that you will begin to see the true success you already possess. This approach is not about taking anything away from you; it's all about giving something back to yourself. In fact, most of this discussion has been based on living a balanced life. However, by living a balanced life, you achieve much more than balance itself. You will gain a richer, more fulfilling life, centered on many key attributes, as illustrated in the following.

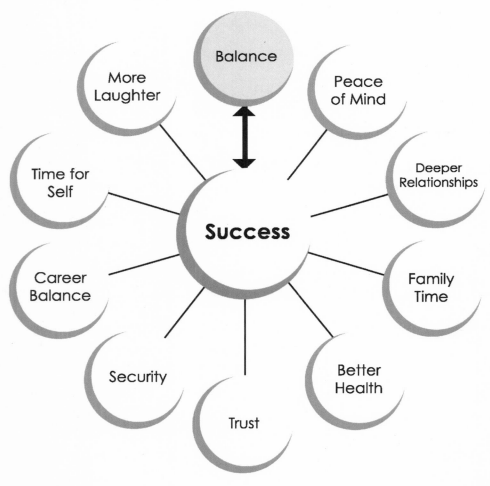

We know real people fight the good fight every day, in spite of the challenges of life. These are people who are doing it in every industry, in every neighborhood and all walks of life. You name the place and country, and real people are striving every day, knowing there is a great possibility that they may never reach the pinnacle of success set by the world's standard. This is truly not a problem, as we now understand, because life is a great deal more than just our vocation or where we sit in society alone. After all, there has to be a better, more complete existence to focus on. We continue to see our friends and families lose their jobs as some corporations struggle to maintain profits at or above par to satisfy Wall Street expectations.

It's time for us to recognize the reality and opportunity associated with our current existence and redefine success through an expanded approach to life.

Folks, I am no expert; nor do I play one on television. However, I had been trapped in a pattern I will refer to as "Wall Street syndrome." I was truly in need of a success makeover.

> "It's through the intentional engagement of your essential areas that you will begin to see the true success you already possess".

11

Wall Street Syndrome

What is Wall Street syndrome? This is a process whereby one's hyper-fixation with achieving traditional success keeps him or her primarily focused on achievements typically associated with obtaining more material gain or advancement in his or her career or status. This fixation is often in conflict with other important elements of an individual's life. For me, this term also highlights a condition wherein the achievements I accomplished were diminished because of the psychological trap I fell into. It kept me believing there was still something bigger and better for me to obtain.

Looking back, this concept was also something that was reared organically during my formative years as a child, throughout my teenage and young-adult years. In fact, the following model illustrates the assimilation process, showing how this becomes a natural part of our being. It's almost like natural selection, as if traditional success chose us, rather than us choosing it. The Wall Street syndrome life model below shows how this process takes over us and how it becomes a natural part of our existence over time. Interestingly enough, it also shows where trouble typically begins to appear, along with its usual impacts. Review the graphic on the next page.

WALL STREET SYNDROME

Infancy 1mon - 5yrs	Childhood 6yrs - 12yrs	Adolecent 13yrs - 19yrs	Adulthood 20yrs - 60yrs	Retirement 55yrs - 70yrs	End of Life 70+yrs
Hyper Dependency	Hyper Dependency	Dependent/ Independance	Total Independance	Prioritization change	Hyper reflection about life
Cry Initiates Action	Learns taught and observed	Self responsibility	Hyper focused on life goals	Lifetime chase and result realized	Limited thinking about traditional success created or not
All Needs Met	Right and wrong distinction	Informative years set	Hyper Dependence on Vacation	Less worry	Abundance of Free time
Unconscious Fulfillment	Heightened desires/ Mine mentality	Hyper focused on needs	Family established/ Family Happenings	Next generation assimilating their own chase	Wonders about legacy will leave
	Unconscious/conscious fulfillment disfinction	Family core values Assimilated	Cognitive sacrifices made: Health, family, friends, work, etc	Path of life solidified	Peace of mind desired
		Peer driven self worth	Competing priorities	State of reflection more prominent	Total need for loved ones
		Ideas shaped by mainstream media	Relational Impacts/ Separation awareness	Hyper focus on loved ones	Question whether fulfillment ever met or not
		Conscious fulfillment prominent	Chase Heavily Invoked	Time recovery	
			Hyper fulfillment Consciousness	See bigger picture	
				Heightened desire for relational fulfillment	

Notice that the model starts out with a hyper dependency in the early years of life to satisfy or fulfill all our needs and wants. Then, as an individual evolves over the life timeline, there is a dependency to independence shift, mitigating the need for assistance from others to depending on oneself to fulfill one's own needs. The interesting catch here is that while you gain greater independence over time personally, your dependence on a vocation or something that will allow you to achieve traditional success becomes the new hyper dependence. The combination of the individual's independence coupled with a hyper dependence for survival and personal fulfillment takes on a whole new meaning, filled with life choices, sacrifices, and priorities in opposition.

Right, wrong, or indifferent, this entire process has been unconsciously endorsed through generational assimilation because the exact same path and behaviors were observed and adopted as a valid way of life from generation to generation.

Let's look at a classic example. Doug, a cable-and-wire salesman, has been at the top of his game for many years, each year outselling his peers by a wide margin. At the start of each year, Doug publicly makes the prediction that he will once again be the top salesman. While no one can deny the remarkable success during Doug's career, his proclamation immediately creates a level of stress. The expectation is that Doug will not only continue to be the best among his peers, but he will achieve higher goals in spite of the year-over-year increase to his target, which has been historically high to begin with.

Doug has enjoyed the benefits of being the top dog in his division with the ability to provide a more-than-comfortable life for his family. However, each year the stress of maintaining that level of success has taken a toll on him and his family, mainly because of the long hours and travel he must maintain to stay on top.

While Doug will do everything in his power to stay on top of his game, he knows it will not be without sacrifice to his family and to himself. Over the years, he has seen the impact on his relationship with his wife, as they seem to be growing further apart. His kids are rapidly growing up right under his nose without any recollection of his regular involvement during their formative years. However, fueled by his chase for success and the responsibility to financially maintain the lifestyle established for his family, Doug will push forward with the notion that he is only as good as his last results, along with the thought that he will eventually be able to spend quality time with his family.

I propose that like Doug, many of us suffer from "Wall Street syndrome." In other words, no matter what level of success we have achieved to date, the expectation is that we must always blow away current results in order to be or remain successful. We have assumed this measuring stick not only for our businesses; we have unconsciously adopted this method for ourselves.

In a capitalistic world where this is an acceptable mode of operation for publicly traded companies or other institutions, this type of measuring stick makes a lot of sense. However, our personal lives are not publicly traded companies and should not be managed by the same standard.

In Doug's example, he was clearly successful. However, his ambition and need to publicly compare his sales ability to that of his peers will eventually lead him to a level of success that will not be achievable, at least not with the kind of balance needed to allow him to experience success in other aspects of his existence. Doug is undoubtedly headed for a life filled with stress and missed opportunities that target the essential areas of his life. We have learned through research that only 1 to 2 percent of people in the world ever experience what traditional success and/or fame has to offer. Given this fact, can we accept that for most of us, giving our very best may only allow us to simply pay the bills, get our kids through college, and go on an occasional vacation? How about if our chase only allowed us to rise to the midlevel ranks of our division or office for a time? Would that be acceptable?

Figuring out how to incorporate the Xente lifestyle not as a limitation of what we can achieve but as a complement to our personal journey can allow us to take a deep breath and appreciate the things we have already or could accomplish as true success. This includes being realistic within ourselves.

Here's a news flash: fame, fortune, or success as defined by the mainstream media isn't predestined for everyone. For those of you who have already accepted that your dream was just that, this is not a collapse in ambition by any stretch of the imagination. This is simply an opportunity to experience living real lives as real people each and every day with dignity, integrity, perseverance, and the knowledge that success encompasses much more than just our bank account or vocation in life. This is about recognition and focusing with a purpose against every essential area of our life, to create a Xente life.

> "Figuring out how to incorporate the Xente lifestyle—
> not as a limitation of what we can achieve but as a
> complement to our personal journey—can allow us to
> take a deep breath and appreciate the things we have
> already or could accomplish as true success."

12

Not Fortune 500 Remnants

Xente is the recognition of simple, everyday people who go through life making an honest living, contributing to society in many different ways. Xente acknowledges the people who may or may not struggle but who continue to gather enough strength to stare life right in the face and to keep doing it with the idea that this may be as good as it gets.

The concept of Xente was born out of a simple idea to help us redefine our view of success, not as a means of promoting a lack of enthusiasm for our life ambitions but to raise up a society where people focus on their complete lives and give themselves credit for all the great things they have and will do.

As much as we have adapted to our current way of thinking, we are not remnants of Fortune 500 firms or an army of one. We are a network of people trying to navigate life with as little trouble and worry as possible. I ask you: are we searching for happiness in all the wrong places, to the exclusion of some very important ones? Or have we willingly accepted that in order to be truly happy, we must have success that is traditionally defined by what we do and/or how much money we earn, without paying any attention to the notable successes we've already accomplished just by living normal, honest lives every day?

Think about the happiest time in your life. I would argue that things were probably much simpler when you first started in your life's journey. It was probably a time when you did not have as much money, material possessions or even wisdom to draw from. I insist that the more you have, the more you want, which contributes to a more stressful or unfulfilled life because we are programmed to want more to be happy. Unfortunately, life experiences have proven time and time again not to work that way. Acquiring more "stuff" is not the key to our happiness.

This idea is not just a gut feeling; it's an economic premise known as the "law of diminishing returns." This premise suggests that as you get more of something (i.e., material possessions), it becomes less valuable. In other words, no matter how great the accomplishments you achieve or the money you earn, it will never be enough, because you will always want to strive for more. Keeping this very concept in mind, could there be a point where you have given all you can and your level of good is already good enough?

Again, we are not Fortune 500 firms. However, consider this for a moment: if we were, we might be on the verge of bankruptcy because we have allowed the critical areas of our "business" (lives) to fall apart—our kids, marriage, spirituality, community; you fill in the blanks with anything other than your vocation, and it has more than likely been impacted.

Folks, we have fostered diminishing returns in our lives with stress beyond measure because we have placed too high a premium in the one area we can only influence but not control.

Now, before you get hung up on this particular view regarding traditional success, this is not an indictment of corporate America—or other firms in the world, for that matter. However, all things need to be put into proper perspective and given due consideration. This way, other areas of our lives can be highlighted or at least brought into greater focus, so the nonwork-related parts of our existence don't fall apart. We all inherently understand this issue but continue to be too wrapped up in the chase to make the change we so desperately need or ultimately desire.

Given the ideas, concepts, and scenarios shared thus far, everything in this book from this point forward will give you all you need to begin your personal success makeover.

I want to introduce you to the Xente lifestyle model. It's a lifestyle model because when you choose to adapt this approach as a normal part of your everyday walk, you will experience true success like never before. This model will begin to connect or reconnect the essential areas of your life, putting you on the path to the kind of happiness your heart and innermost ambitions have been longing for. The good news is that you are already equipped with everything you need to make a difference.

> "I insist that the more you have, the more you want, which contributes to a more stressful or unfulfilled life because we are programmed to want more to be happy."

13

Xente Lifestyle Model

The Xente Lifestyle Model is a balanced approach to six essential focus areas in your life. When you manage your life focusing on the following essential areas functioning with balance or intentional engagement as a primary outcome, your life will begin to reflect the kind of success that will pay dividends for a lifetime with potential generational impacts. The focus areas are:

- **Your family** (immediate and extended family members)
- **Your significant other** (or spouse as a distinct sub-element of your family)
- **Your friends**
- **Your community** (immediate neighbors, neighborhood, church- and/or community-based organization, etc.)

- **Your vocation** (job, area of expertise, talent, etc.)
- **Yourself**

Always remember that too much focus in any one essential area to the exclusion of any others will create an imbalance. Being intentional about your approach to each of these essential areas is vital to experience the kind of success you want out of your life's journey.

Now, you may be asking how did we arrive at these particular essential focus areas, and why are they so important? Let's take a closer look at each one.

Your family: Interestingly enough, we say that this essential area represents one of our greatest priorities.

However, many kids spend significant time at local daycares or with other family members, due to parental work responsibilities, which are initiated by our need to support our family and the lifestyles we maintain.

This is very understandable. However, when we get the opportunity to spend quality time with our kids, we are often too tired to really enjoy or connect with them and other family members in a meaningful way.

This is an area I can speak about firsthand. I was so busy "taking care of the kids" through my disproportionate efforts on the job that I missed some of the best times of their lives—only to look back and ask *was it really worth it?*

This essential area may offer the greatest legacy one could have because it may change generations to come if we learn to connect with our kids with a greater level of commitment.

In addition, our extended families fall into the same category of missed time; they are also a very important part of our lives. In fact, a greater focus in this particular essential area will allow you to facilitate meaningful connections with other members of your family—whether your connection is for the care and consideration of aging parents or providing mentorship to younger family members outside of your household (e.g., niece or nephew) or simply spending time with siblings.

We must embrace the idea that we can change the paradigm that consumes us by making some very simple adjustments. This is reflected in the Xente Life model on the next page.

This particular model is similar to the Wall Street syndrome model and illustrates the same level of dependency at each life stage. The difference is that an individual's ability to introduce the Xente lifestyle value system into his or her life will help facilitate the ability to feel successful or reach a sense of fulfillment along his or her entire life's journey.

XENTE LIFE IMPACT

Infancy 1mon - 5yrs	Childhood 6yrs - 12yrs	Adolecent 13yrs - 19yrs	Adulthood 20yrs - 60yrs	Retirement 55yrs - 70yrs	End of Life 70+yrs
Hyper Dependency	Hyper Dependency	Dependent/ Independance	Total Independence	Balanced in life maintained not consumed with the clock	Hyper state of Reflection about life
Cry Initiates Action	Learns taught and observed	Self responsibility with intentional guidance	Focused on life goals but balanced with family needs	Realization of everything life has to offer	Limited thinking about traditional success created
All Needs Met	Relational core values emphasized	Informative years set	Dependence on Vocation balance with strong support network	Clearly sees the fruits of labor and love	Peace of mind
Unconscious Fulfillment	Heightened desires/ Mine mentality	Focused on own needs but balanced with needs of others	Family establised/ Family Happenings	Next generation assimilating benefits of living a complete life	Surrounded by loved ones
	Unconscious/conscious fulfillment distinction	Family core values Assimilated	Hyper consciousness of impacts to every aspect of life	Path of life solidified	An incredible legacy of connectedness and love
		Peer driven self worth	Relational impacts minimized by Intentionality	State of reflection more prominent	Fulfillment of A Complete Life
		Ideas shaped by mainstream media balanced by family core values	Chase in sight not all consuming	Hyper focus on loved ones	"Xente Success"
		Conscious fulfillment prominent	Continual fulfillment realized future goals sill in alignment with other goals	Abundance of time to share	
				The bigger picture even brighter than originally conceived	

They say the best things in life are free, and the Xente lifestyle harnesses this premise simply because you do not have to go and find it; it is often right in front of you. Interestingly enough, the same form of assimilation takes place with one key difference.

In the Xente Life model, the behaviors assimilated are connected to balance and prioritization that takes an individual's complete life elements into consideration. The Xente lifestyle still focuses on the importance of a vocation, but it does not advocate a heightened focus in that area alone. In fact, it highlights focus and balance as a way of making you even more effective, thereby creating the kind of fulfillment that is maintained throughout a lifetime versus some unknown point in the future.

This concept is very simple to apply and will begin to take incredible shape in your life, even as you make gradual but consistent adjustments.

Now that you see the potential impacts based on your current choices and the new Xente options, please keep both models in mind as you review the remaining scenarios. It will help clearly paint the picture of the issues and opportunities that exist for your life moving forward.

As an example, let's look at a common scenario. Sally is a single working mother with two young children. She is often tired after a long day of work and would much rather get the essentials done with the kids every evening (like dinner and homework) and then slip in a movie or let them play video games until it's time to head off to bed. She then starts the whole thing all over the next day.

The kids have continually pleaded with Sally to sit with them and play a game or simply spend quality time laughing and joking together. However, Sally has explained that she is too tired or busy to do anything and excuses herself to complete other tasks in the home. (Notice that she is too tired but goes off to do other tasks.) This has become a regular occurrence in her household, so much so that her kids have begun mocking her responses about being too tired or busy.

While Sally's challenges of being a single mom and engaging with her kids are understandable, the constant denial of Sally's bonding with her kids may become a challenge after a prolonged period of time. Things like acting out in school or poor relationships with other children or just being defiant to authority figures may become another reality for Sally's children, thereby creating additional challenges to what already exists.

However, with gradual Xente Life adjustments, Sally has an opportunity to be proactive and plan with a purpose, to let her children know they matter. This can happen in multiple ways, but one example might be Sally evaluating how she is currently allocating her time and establishing a priority that keeps her kids' need to bond with her in focus. Being thoughtful about this alone will also allow Sally to plan in advance, so this all-important connection can be made. Perhaps there is an incentive for the kids to help Sally with some of the chores, to help facilitate making time with one another or even bonding while completing the chores.

The results will be Sally getting some help and the kids getting that all-important time with their mother. For Sally, making the right adjustment to bring additional balance to her life is clearly a positive impact, as depicted on the Xente Life model.

Your Significant Other/Spouse: This essential area is specifically separated from the core family essential area because this is often one of the most challenging areas of any connection you will make (considering the fact that divorce is still a major issue facing Americans today). I have heard it time and time again that people put the needs of the kids or family first. How do they typically do that? Through their jobs. That means this essential area may be a distant third place, considering in the list of priorities, the kids typically get top billing over the parents.

This makes for another challenging area to leverage outside of the Xente model. Through my own experience, I know that when my spouse and I were operating as one, everything else seemed to be reasonably manageable. However, when we neglected our relationship in favor of other areas of our lives, we were more frequently at odds. This alone establishes a strong case for why your relationship with your spouse or significant other is an area to place a great deal of importance or attention.

Let's look at this scenario involving a couple named Jacob and Linda. Jacob has been married to Linda for twelve years. Both have full-time jobs, and they have three kids in grade school. Between the two of them, Jacob and Linda are either carpooling with other working parents to get the children off to evening activities or community sports, doing household chores, preparing dinner, or sitting with the kids doing homework. However, at least once per week, Jacob is able to connect with the guys in his bowling league, while Linda continues to keep pace with the kids and their activities.

Linda has shared with Jacob that she is concerned because they rarely spend any dedicated time together like going on dates, walking like they used to, or simply talking at the end of the night without falling asleep on each other.

While Jacob agrees, he insists that things will eventually get better—but doesn't offer any suggestions to deal with Linda's present concern. Over time, life becomes busier, and the opportunity to get the much-needed quality time together continues to be a distant memory for Linda. As a result, she becomes progressively withdrawn and short with Jacob. This was only the start of the issues they experienced as their intimate moments together became less frequent. On the occasions when they could connect, Sally often complained about not feeling well or just flat-out refused any advances made by Jacob.

In this scenario, life with a young family and full-time jobs can be tough to balance. However, like the other tasks in Jacob and Linda's lives, setting the right priority to meet Linda's needs is nothing more than a scheduling occurrence. Meeting her needs is not a complicated process. In fact, a small amount of attention and consideration on a consistent basis will allow Linda to feel appreciated and get the much-needed downtime to produce a happier, healthier relationship with herself, Jacob, and the rest of the family. This is living a Xente life.

Your Friends: This is an essential focus area because no matter what stage of life you are in, friendships represent a key component of our history, as well as an important link to our identity. Interestingly, as certain aspects of our lives begin to evolve, our relationships with our friends begin to give way to the other priorities of life. So much so that we unconsciously and sometimes consciously allow our friendships to take a back seat because we are too busy or only have enough bandwidth for the items we consider really vital to our daily existence. I get this, and most of us would as well, but I would argue that an active, meaningful friendship or two can be particularly vital to one's life, whether married or single.

Case in point, Lilly has been married for a number of years and recently experienced the hardship of divorce. The difficulty of this experience caused Lilly to miss significant time with family, friends, and work—a clear sign she was suffering from depression over all that had happened. Prior to Lilly's current situation, she was always known to be the life of the party, always willing to help others. Lilly was no stranger to divorce because she was a product of divorce and had a friend or two who had also gone through a similar circumstance. In fact, during that time, Lilly spent a great many occasions consoling her friends and letting them know that everything would be okay. She was right;

everything did work out. Unfortunately, she did not have the same enthusiasm when dealing with her own divorce.

The overwhelming emotions that resulted from the immediate separation, anger, hurt, and eventual sadness weighed heavily on Lilly. But because of the unfailing commitment of her two friends whom she once consoled in their circumstances, Lilly received the same thoughtfulness and nurturing. This included them taking her out to dinner, providing a shoulder to cry on during her roughest moments, and simply calling to check on her each day when they could not physically be there with her. These connections eventually led her back to a healthy, functioning frame of mind. Being there as a friend, regardless of any efforts to push you away or reject you due to life's circumstances, is Xente!

Your Community: If you think you struggle for time with your spouse, the kids, or your friends, then this essential area hasn't a chance in hell. This area is a challenge because some of us may not view it as an essential area of our lives, simply because we are so used to looking out for ourselves. However, many people would tell you they have had, at one point or another, the desire to give something meaningful back to their community or even on a broader scale. Yet many churches, community centers, and volunteer organizations struggle to get meaningful involvement from the masses, despite our alleged desire to give back.

Even as an alternative, if we look at our community as being our next-door neighbor or even the people we may see at the local grocery store, we find it difficult to engage or connect with one another in the simplest ways.

This essential area is very important because it allows us to look outside of our typical area of concern or responsibility (ourselves), with the idea of giving something back with no strings attached. Again going back to the Wall Street syndrome model, it is part of our life conditioning to go out and fend for ourselves. While we are typically taught it is good to share as kids, we are rarely taught that giving back to our community or our environment on a consistent basis actually perpetuates a healthy way of living a complete life. A regular dose of this essential area helps us to increase our overall compassion and goodwill toward others outside of our normal community of family and friends.

In fact, once upon a time this was the essence of the concept "it takes a village to raise a child." This simple premise compelled involvement by the people who lived in the community not to turn a blind eye if they saw any child—not just their own—doing something inappropriate.

They intervened because it was the right thing to do, and it reinforced good morals in and outside of the home. In that same way, it takes a village of normal, everyday people like you and me to get involved in our communities also to make a difference. Some call it being a good neighbor; others may refer to it as paying it forward. No matter what you call it, the impact of your active connection can only contribute to the improvement or well-being of your community.

Take Bill, for example. He has lived in his community of Hanover Heights, Illinois, for most of his life. Bill has always wanted to do something meaningful within his community. While Bill maintains a busy schedule between his full- and part-time jobs, his desire to contribute to his community has continued to grow over the years, as he often reflects on his own childhood story.

Bill recalls that when he was a little boy, his father had lost his job one Christmas holiday season and was struggling to keep food on the table for his family. It was a tough year, and the fact that they could hardly keep food on the table meant this particular Christmas was going to be less than merry. Barely understanding why his family was struggling so much, Bill conceded there would be nothing to unwrap under their scarcely lit tree that year, and he was right.

Christmas Eve had come and gone, and the entire family finally gathered at the dinner table on Christmas, eating mac and cheese and a canned ham with sweet potatoes (probably compliments of the local food pantry).

While there were no gifts to open, the family enjoyed their time together, playing games and laughing throughout Christmas Day. Right before dinner was complete, there was a knock at the door.

Expecting no one to stop by, everyone was curious as to who it could be. Upon opening the front door, Bill's father exhaled as their next-door neighbor and his wife presented him with a stack of wrapped Christmas gifts and enough groceries to feed the family for a week. This was an incredible surprise and a miracle by Bill's estimation. Every one of his brothers and sisters received his or her very own gift. There was even a gift for Mom and Dad, he recalls. The impact of that act of compassion by that neighbor for Bill and his family made a lasting impression on his life.

As a result, every year for the last ten years, Bill collects donated food and wrapped gifts to provide assistance for up to a hundred needy families at Christmastime, delivering the same gift he and his family once received that tough Christmas season.

No one has to go to the extent that Bill continues to do, to make a difference in the lives around them. However, you never know how your connection to serve or be there for someone else will have a meaningful impact on this world. Stepping outside of yourself for the greater good of others is Xente.

Your Vocation: Whether you are focused on your job, education, or a specific talent, this essential area is and always will be a very important element in your life. For most, this area is often viewed as the key to unlocking the path to success and all of the fringe benefits that go along with it. This is clearly the measuring stick by which most define whether they have arrived or not. However, in many cases we have made this such an all-encompassing focus in our lives that consequently, this area has become the ultimate excuse for neglecting all other essential areas. Sadly enough, most of us have made this an acceptable mode of operation.

This area also represents by far the greatest opportunity for balance. For instance, it has been said that people are so overworked that our culture is creating a lack of productivity because most of us are too exhausted to realize that we are sometimes less productive than our actual potential.

To illustrate this point, I want to recall a story shared with me by Carlita, a longtime colleague. Carlita is your typical type-A personality who lives to work. It was common for Carlita to work an average of seventy to eighty hours a week. After all, as she puts it, "I am not married and have no real commitments to speak of at this point in my life."

In fact, she subscribes to the philosophy that she will work as hard as she can and save enough money so that when she does finally slow down enough to have a family, she will be financially set. Until then, Carlita is rarely upset over missed vacations or her less-than-meaningful personal relationships outside of work.

However, Carlita recently shared with me that she has been experiencing problems with sleeping at night, and her short term memory has been failing her—even to the extent that she has missed some pretty important meetings, despite their being on her calendar.

The scariest moment she recalls was her sitting at her desk one morning and wondering how in the heck she got to work that day; she actually could not remember waking up, showering, getting dressed, leaving her home, or even driving to work. Really? Balance! We have the opportunity to become better stewards of our vocations if we can learn that balance actually makes us better or more efficient.

Carlita was obviously way out of balance with her life. Living a Xente lifestyle would allow her to bring into focus other essential areas and create a healthier, more balanced, and connected life. This would enable her to experience life versus blazing through it without remembering it. Keep in mind, time has rarely captured anyone on their deathbed stating that they wished for more time spent in the office.

In fact, nine out of ten individuals at the summit of their life say if given the ability to go back in time, they would make a greater effort to live a more balanced life, taking full advantage of every aspect of their existence. This is the very basis for a Xente lifestyle.

Yourself: It's mind-boggling that we never fully appreciate the challenge this essential area represents in our lives. However, this offers another chance to regulate our lives and gain more balance. As Maslow's hierarchy of needs suggests, humans will always seek to fulfill their most basic needs of life until they are satisfied (needs like nourishment, safety, relationships, image, and achievement). We tend to impute a great sacrifice on our well-being in order to chase traditional success or our ultimate dream. We typically do this under the assumption that everything will work out in the end and everyone will be happier once we get there.

This couldn't be a more false statement. Putting aside the negative impact to every essential area surrounding you, your literal unintentional self-sacrifice can and frequently does take its toll on you, rendering you physically exhausted, ineffective, and emotionally detached.

For example, let's look at a man we will call Bruce. Bruce has been an independent, over-the-road truck driver for twenty years. Bruce's job is very stressful because his ability to get additional work and bonuses relies heavily on him delivering his loads on time and without any losses or damages to product.

Being a small, independent, over-the-road driver, there is only one vehicle representing his company. Because of Bruce's single marital status, he is often on the road taking as many jobs as he can, pushing his physical abilities and sometimes bending the laws—with regard to the amount of time he spends behind the wheel to earn as much money as possible. As a result of the years of sitting behind the wheel of his truck and overeating fast food, Bruce has gained significant weight and often complains about low energy and excessive aches and pains, which includes tightness in his chest from time to time. Despite these recurring issues, Bruce continues to push himself with minimum sleep, which he covers up by consuming energy drinks and capsules.

This example clearly shows that even with Bruce's own physical complaints and the laws that were designed to help keep him and others safe, Bruce's focus on earning as much money as possible has become a priority—even beyond his own well-being.

While we can understand some of the challenges that can exist with high-stress jobs—or any job, for that matter—we also know that without a general care or concern for oneself, there is no sustainable way to maintain any of it. While it was easy to point out the issues in Bruce's scenario, this is a very common way of life for many of us. Living a Xente life where you focus or take time out for yourself creates a path to stability and well-being. One thing about it: you won't be able to impact any area of your life if you do not have your health and sanity.

As you can see, these essential areas make up the core of who we are meant to be. There is no way around it; we are all connected. Each one of the essential areas is like a vital link connecting the chain of our existence.

To deny any one of these is to deny a critical element of life to coexist within us. This would be like getting on a rollercoaster ride, knowing that a critical stabilizing mechanism was missing. Who would be willing to proceed on that uncertain ride? To even respond to this question would be ridiculous, let alone taking the ride.

You are the ultimate essential element because you are the point at which all other essential elements converge. To intentionally engage all essential elements is the key to a more successful, happier life.

I once met an elderly woman named Lin, who had been retired from teaching for about ten years. I actually met Lin while flying on a business trip to New Orleans. Lin was a soft-spoken woman with a very inviting disposition. During the flight, she began telling me all about her family and her years as a teacher. That lifestyle, which included having most weekends and summers off, allowed her to do many things in her life like take vacations, spend time with family and friends, and even volunteer on a consistent basis.

Despite the loss of her husband a few years back, she talked about how they had enjoyed a wonderful life together and how they'd enjoyed just being the best of friends. She said there wasn't anything they didn't share with one another, even as they raised three children (two of whom are teachers and the other a manager in corporate America).

Lin also talked about how much she enjoyed family reunions (hence the trip to New Orleans) because it allowed her to relive and create many great memories with loved ones. As a retiree, Lin spent a lot of her time volunteering at hospitals and her local senior community center. It seemed as though Lin lived the ideal life. As time rapidly passed us by for the nearly two-and-a-half-hour flight, Lin effortlessly managed to keep me captivated.

It also became apparent to me that anything I could fit in edgewise about my busy life of business paled in comparison to the life she lived and continues to live.

As the captain announced preparations for our descent into New Orleans, I asked Lin what she considered the most important elements of a happy and successful life. She smiled sincerely at me and said, "Take the time to experience every aspect of your life; you only get one shot at it." I could only smile back and say *yes*. Making sure you are taking the time to intentionally connect with each of the essential areas of your life is the essence of a Xente lifestyle!

Now that you understand why these essential areas were chosen, let's take a closer look at how to put all of these components together and into action through this simple yet effective process.

> "Nine out of ten individuals at the summit of their life say if given the ability to go back in time, they would make a greater effort to live a more balanced life, taking full advantage of every aspect of their existence."

C.A.RE

Connect, Activate, and Reconnect

14

The Xente Care
(C.A.RE) Process

Do not accept your current way of living, falling prey to this crazy rat race; you can begin to experience relative success now and in all of the areas of your life by utilizing a simple process where you simply *connect, activate,* and *reconnect (C.A.RE).*

Friends, this is not a ten-step program or a complicated thing to understand; in fact, it is very simple. This is something that can be easily completed between wives and husbands, parents and children, friends, bosses and employees, church leadership and its congregation, and any other scenario where connecting with others matters. The premise is that everyone is connecting and that everyone involved can live out the joys and successes that arise when they connect with intentionality or a specific purpose. Adopting this movement will help to perpetuate a sense of well-being, giving people new hope and success right where they are in life. The results can generate relative success and positive impacts for generations to come, as depicted in the Xente Life model.

If any of the scenarios shared resonates with you on any level, you deserve the opportunity to regain or recharge your life without delay. Experience success now by adopting a Xente Lifestyle, not only for a more balanced, productive existence but a happier life!

> "Do not accept your current way of living, falling prey to this crazy rat race; you can begin to experience relative success now and in all of the areas of your life."

15

Sample Xente Profiles

If you are still wondering how you fit into all of this, if this lifestyle could really work or even apply to your life, review the following profiles and see if any of these life summations connect with you. If they do, then you have the perfect opportunity to live a Xente Lifestyle right now!

Corporate Achiever: You are an individual who has always known what you have wanted. You have succeeded in just about everything you have done, and you make no apologies for your quest to be successful.

Public Safety: You are an individual who puts your life on the line every day. You make it your business to do the things that most people would cringe or run away from.

Public Servant: You are an individual who works in a municipal, city, state, or federal position. You live a life of constant reminders that it is your job to serve to the highest standard of quality and integrity. Your job is often thankless, but it is your job to give service with a smile.

Stay-at-Home Advocate: You are the CEO, CFO, COO, and every other role you can think of. You are the individual who, despite any dreams of your own, sees the caring for your family as paramount. You sacrifice your wants and sometimes your needs to make sure your family is cared for first. Perhaps the most thankless job of all in the list, you are often tired and overworked, but you keep pushing forward every day, just because it is what you live for.

Parents Again: You are the grandmothers and grandfathers who have assumed the occupational caregiver roles for your kid's children. You too once had dreams but have long realized that these dreams were just that. Trying to survive in your retirement but assuming the role of parent, you too are tired; but with a deep sense of love and empathy for your kids, you are back in the rat race again.

Spiritual Advisors: You are the individuals destined to carry the burden of your flock here on earth. Your life is filled with chaos, trying to be everything to everyone, and you still feel like you fail to hit the mark. Your ultimate goal is that everyone will see the light; unfortunately your sheep are too caught up in the field, trying to find the best patch of grass to graze upon. Your energy is constantly being drained, trying to deal with people chasing dreams that don't matter, while at times you wonder: am I in the right place, or how did I get here?

Healthcare Service Providers: You are the people who constantly see the results of what imbalance will do to an individual. You are the interesting ones because you understand clearly all the things you need to do but most often ignore them because of your own busy lives.

Often working long days on shifting schedules or double shifts to help fill the demand, you find yourself totally spent after meeting the needs of the people you serve and the remainder of your personal life, but you keep moving forward, exemplifying the Hippocratic oath you may have sworn to once upon a time.

Retail Warriors: You are the broadest category of individuals, who run the gamut of our population, representing every culture, age, sex, and disposition. You often struggle to make ends meet, either through the lack of hours scheduled or the fact that this is your second or third part-time job.

You may not even like what you are doing, but you continue doing it because it does meet a need, even if it is a small portion of what you ultimately need in the end.

The Student: You are the individual who still believes in dreams. You see what you do as a means to an agonizing end. Generally speaking, you do this not because you like it but because you believe that when you accomplish your educational goal, opportunities will open up for you or it will be the catalyst that will propel you on the road to success.

Trades, Technicians, and Manufacturing Individuals: You are the individuals who take your physical abilities to the max every day. Guarded by the clock, you push yourselves to meet certain tasks and duties with precision. You have the best opportunity to recognize success because when you clock out for the day, your job is done until tomorrow; you most often don't have the ability to take your job with you. Given that, your motivation is productivity and getting as much done as possible.

Military—Our Returning Heroes: You are the individuals who willingly chose to serve our country despite the crazy times we are living in. You have seen many of our patriots pay the ultimate price for our liberty. Some of you have returned from active duty, trying to figure out if there is a place for you, struggling to get to that place of normal, everyday existence. When asked about your service, you often say you would do it all over again if needed.

Educators/Trainers: For so many years, you are the individuals who undertake the unenviable task of being the majority ruler over our children's minds. Your role is incredible because it is you who continue to be there as we grow in life, until we are released into this world. Having accomplished your goal of being able to mold the minds of every walk of life in some form or fashion, you live a modest life, filled with the typical ups and downs; you continue to muster the courage and strength each day to show the minds of the world that you really care about their development.

While some of you will easily identify yourselves with the Xente sample profiles referenced above, there are others who do not see themselves in this manner. In fact, some may have a more difficult time classifying themselves at all. However, their behavior or disposition about life in general provides a basis for describing them. I offer the following abstract examples to highlight my point. Keep in mind there are many others, but I have observed these two most often.

The Dreamer: You are the individual who everyone else sees as either unmotivated or a free spirit. You truly believe that work is not the most important thing in the world. You are the one who believes in true love and that dreams really do come true, especially if you believe in them. You are most often identified with your incredible talent and are hopeful that one day you will get your big break to show the world how amazing you are.

Everyday Survivor: You are the individual who has long given up on your ultimate dream. In fact, you are doing whatever you can to survive without being too selective about whether you are going to like your job or not, as long as it's steady and pays the bills. You take life as it comes, accepting your path without being too high or too low about life in general. Your motto tends to be "it is what it is."

These examples are by no means an exhaustive representation of those who have the ability to live a Xente lifestyle. That said, no matter where you land or how you classify yourself, everyday people in every vocation or chosen path in life have their challenges and opportunities. It is also a fact that success can be found in every one of the profiles shared, as well as the ones I did not share. I will also go out on a limb and say that most of us at some point or another will struggle with balance; this notion alone makes most of us prime candidates for a success makeover.

> "Xente is the recognition of simple, everyday people who go through life making an honest living, contributing to society in many different ways".

16

Xente Lifestyle Goal

The beauty of the Xente lifestyle is that the success you can and will experience is not a set of predetermined outcomes on a list. In fact, your success experience can be as unique as your fingerprint. After all, your life is different than mine, your neighbors', friends', or even your spouse or significant other's. We are uniquely different to enhance the connections we make in life, not to create a perpetual point of friction. Given the traditional success view that we have assimilated to, we have also created a self-induced paradox, which keeps us from doing the very thing we were designed to do: connecting in meaningful ways.

It's time to adopt a more realistic view of what success can be in your life. I am talking about being happy with the everyday things accomplished in your life's journey, not what you have observed in someone else's life or seen in the mainstream media. Contrary to popular belief, while everyone is created equally, we are not the same, so the results produced in one person's life will be different than another's. However, everyone can experience relative success and continue to grow from there.

The reality of life is you can't achieve any type of success overnight, no matter who you are. It's the intentional baby steps you take that will make the difference in your particular journey. If it were not so, how could people raise a family, make it through college, make new friends, serve in communities, or learn to take joy in nonmaterialistic things? How could we find joy in being able to spend quality time with loved ones, avoiding a stressful life, or being able to love our jobs but not have them consume our entire waking lives? What if you could manage all the essential areas of your life with the kind of balance that brings peace and joy to not only you but the people you connect with?

No matter what essential areas you decide to bring into focus, when you implement the Xente C.A.RE process, you will begin to experience realistic success and happiness. Now let's take a look at the C.A.RE process.

Connect

With the current pace of life, many people have abandoned the lost art of connecting in a real location face-to-face, to invest real time with one another, and replaced it with message tagging or fly-by virtual relationships. In fact, most people today have become overly effective at hiding behind these tools of convenience, perpetuating superficial connections. The premise behind connecting is to encourage authentic interactions through meaningful events. This does not have to be complex; just remember not to make any one essential area all consuming.

Some examples of true connecting might be a night out on the town with a loved one, going to the park and playing ball with the kids, seeing a concert with a friend, or even making time to make phone calls to younger or elderly extended family members. Establishing a pattern of authentic interacting is very important because it shows your commitment and it lets others experience your intentions concerning your time with them. If the essential area chosen is focused on yourself, then some self-reflection time may be in order, allowing you to think about the impact to your own well-being. This lifestyle approach brings restoration across the essential areas of life that you choose to focus on.

Remember, success is not only about your vocation, so your goals will focus in multiple areas. Balance is essential, as it reminds you that there are other important areas in your life (hence the six essential focus areas). Now that you understand the premise behind *Connect*, all you have to do is choose an essential focus area to impact and then activate it.

Activate

When activating your essential focus area, you must simply carry out or perform the committed event or action associated with the selected focus area.

No matter how you choose to activate the essential areas of your life, just know that the efforts you extend will begin to help transform the way you think about the world around you, and more importantly, how people begin to respond to your intentional efforts. Taking it a step further, you might dare to ask your connections what would make your forthcoming events together even more fulfilling.

Reconnect

Once you have activated that essential area for the chosen connection, you want to keep your next connection in sight. This connection does not have to focus on the same essential element. In fact, it makes the most sense to mix it up and focus on a whole new area, given that balance is your main objective. It is also very important to get your next connection lined up because it keeps you aware that success is just another connection away. Keep in mind that it is easy for us to develop routines that are very repetitive or mundane, so don't let this happen to you. (This is the making of a mini rat race.)

Take the opportunity to really get creative in your approach to your connections, as it can begin to make a difference in your quality of life. It will also give the individuals you are connecting to something to look forward to. Being very intentional and thoughtful about what you do in this process will set an important tone. You don't want to create thoughtless activity that simply goes through the motions or that will not allow you to experience the success that meaningful connections can bring.

My desired outcome for you is this: by the time you are done with this book, you will have some practical ways to get your life's journey back on track. This is gut-check time! Are you with me? Good!

For each of the essential focus areas provided, I will share some simple but meaningful examples on how you can connect, activate, and reconnect your way into experiencing success today. I have also developed Xentelife mobile applications downloaded via the Apple or Google stores that are designed to help you facilitate connecting to all of the highlighted essential areas in an easy-to-use manner.

This will help you to build and sustain the exact success mentioned here.

You may already be doing well in certain essential areas of your life, so start with applying the focus where you need it most. To help you further understand what areas you may want to focus on immediately, I have provided a series of short assessments. They will help you reflect on the current condition of a particular essential focus area as it relates to your own life. Keep in mind that the assessments will not point out every opportunity for success, but they will allow you to reflect on the results of your personal effort for a given area connected to your life's journey.

> "The premise behind connecting is to encourage authentic interactions through meaningful events."

17

Xente Assessments and Scoring Scale

The purpose of the following Xente assessments is to give you an idea of how you are doing with respect to the Xente essential areas related to your life. (Some questions or statements may ask you to rate how you think others feel.) These assessments will give you an indication of where you stand at a macro level. However, we also want to be sensitive to the fact that there are other factors that may impact your particular situation.

The result of each assessment is not calculated using a complicated algorithm; it is calculated on the total summation of your honest responses to each of the questions and statements.

Essentially, this is you looking in the mirror and capturing what you see and feel in black and white. This will also serve as your initial step to analyzing areas where you need proactive focus.

The questions and statements for each of the essential areas were chosen based on typical interactions needed to cultivate success in your life. Keep in mind that once you have analyzed your results and begun to move forward on your new journey, the outcome generated for each of the essential areas of your life will be determined by your level of commitment. Not the kind of commitment that becomes all-consuming in the beginning and then fizzles out like some fad diet, but the kind of commitment that is given and sustained when you sincerely care for or value something.

With all of this in mind, rate each of the statements as it applies to you based on a scale of one to five:

- 1 = Strongly disagree
- 2 = Disagree
- 3 = Neutral
- 4 = Agree
- 5 = Strongly agree

At the end of each Xente assessment, add your scores for all questions, and use the following scale to determine your current state of connecting.

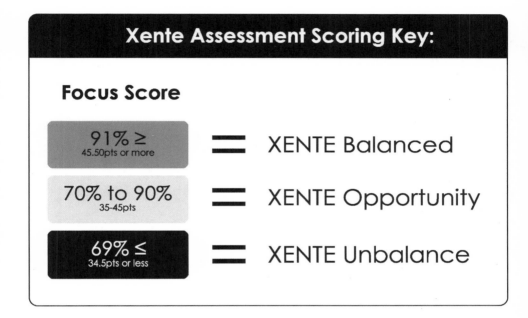

Note: When you fall into the "Xente Balanced" level, you still need to continue to work at this to keep successes thriving.

18

Take Xente Assessments

Vocation (Sample Assessment)	
Complete the following survey by placing a score next to each question that best describes your answer. Use the following 5 point scale range of 1 to 5: (1 = Strongly Disagree, 2= Disagree, 3= Neutral, 4= Agree and 5 = Strongly Agree to)	**Score**
1. You maintain a good balance between your work, hobbies and home life.	4
2. Your work motto would best be described as "working to live" versus "living to work".	3
3. You find a balance of joy and fulfillment in your work goals when compared to goals at home.	2
4. You use your yearly vacation/time off available to you from your employer.	4
5. You get along with everyone at your place of employment or school.	5
6. You take on personal responsibility for ensuring that everything is done correctly in your department.	3
7. You tend to be more ambitious than your friends or colleagues.	3
8. You are the "go to" person whenever anything important is needed.	4
9. You tend to be the one to volunteer for any type of assignment or special project.	4
10. In your work or school environment, people see you as a valued member of the team.	4
Total Score Xente Opportunity ▶	36

Note: Please reference scale on previous page

Self	
Complete the following survey by placing a score next to each question that best describes your answer. Use the following 5 point scale range of 1 to 5: (1 = Strongly Disagree, 2= Disagree, 3= Neutral, 4= Agree and 5 = Strongly Agree to)	**Score**
1. You feel you maintain a good level of energy throughout the day.	
2. You feel you have an appropriate amount of time to do the things you want to do every day.	
3. You get the right amount of exercise and would consider yourself healthy.	
4. You have a healthy balance for needs of others compared to your own needs.	
5. You feel best when you are "giving" rather than "receiving".	
6. You consider your current life to be positive.	
7. You feel you have a specific talent(s) that can help you achieve success.	
8. You feel content in all areas of your life.	
9. When something good happens to someone else, you feel happy for that individual.	
10. When you look in the mirror, you like what you see.	
Total Score	

Significant Other or Spouse

Complete the following survey by placing a score next to each question that best describes your answer. Use the following 5 point scale range of 1 to 5: (1 = Strongly Disagree, 2= Disagree, 3= Neutral, 4= Agree and 5 = Strongly Agree to)	Score
1. You regularly have meaningful and engaging conversations with your significant other.	
2. Your conversations with your significant other tend to be positive.	
3. You and your significant other regularly engage in outings together (friends, family, date, etc.)	
4. You communicate with your significant other multiple times throughout the day.	
5. After being away from your significant other during the day, you always engage them with an affectionate greeting when you reconnect.	
6. You are actively engaged and aware of your significant other's daily schedule.	
7. You proactively engage in kind and positive acts to please your significant other.	
8. Your physical encounters with your spouse tend to be heartfelt passion vs. duty.	
9. You are happier when spending time with your spouse at home instead of being at work.	
10. You often think about spending quality time with your significant other.	
Total Score	

Friends	Score
Complete the following survey by placing a score next to each question that best describes your answer. Use the following 5 point scale range of 1 to 5: (1 = Strongly Disagree, 2= Disagree, 3= Neutral, 4= Agree and 5 = Strongly Agree to)	
1. You regularly initiate meaningful or engaging conversations with your friend(s).	
2. Your conversations with your friend(s) are mostly positive.	
3. You are more likely to participate in an outing with a friend(s) versus being alone.	
4. You are likely to initiate a conversation with a friend you have not heard from in a while.	
5. You are likely to make time for a friend after a long day at work if they needed to talk.	
6. Besides your necessary daily needs, you prioritize your friends needs over those of your own.	
7. You proactively perform acts of kindness to please your friends.	
8. Holiday and birthday giving is heartfelt vs. a duty.	
9. You are happier when you are spending time with your friends vs. being at work.	
10. You take time to actively learn about your friend(s) family, social endeavors, work, etc.	
Total Score	

Family	Score
Complete the following survey by placing a score next to each question that best describes your answer. Use the following 5 point scale range of 1 to 5: (1 = Strongly Disagree, 2= Disagree, 3= Neutral, 4= Agree and 5 = Strongly Agree to)	
1. You stay in touch with and participate in family events when they happen.	
2. You regularly make your family event a priority over all other events on your calendar.	
3. You enjoy spending undistracted time with your family members.	
4. You keep most, if not all, promises made to your family.	
5. If asked, your family would say you enjoy spending time with them.	
6. If asked, your family members would agree that they are important in your life.	
7. If asked, your family would say that your work is in balance with the rest of your life.	
8. You enjoy going out and socializing with your family rather than staying home watching TV, etc.	
9. Regardless of how you feel, you always make time for your family when they need you.	
10. You are likely to host family gatherings in your home before other family members.	
Total Score	

Children

Complete the following survey by placing a score next to each question that best describes your answer. Use the following 5 point scale range of 1 to 5: (1 = Strongly Disagree, 2= Disagree, 3= Neutral, 4= Agree and 5 = Strongly Agree to)	Score
1. You handle/schedule or are aware of most activities associated with your children.	
2. You make your children's events a priority over all other events on your calendar.	
3. You spend undistracted quality time with your children on a regular basis.	
4. You keep most, if not all, of your promises to your children.	
5. Your children would say you enjoy spending time with them.	
6. Your children would agree that they are an important aspect of your daily life.	
7. Your children believe you have a good balance between work and family.	
8. You would rather do something with your children than sit in solitude when they are around you.	
9. You always make time to answer questions for your children.	
10. You have a plan to help your children become successful adults.	
Total Score	

Vocation (Job)

Complete the following survey by placing a score next to each question that best describes your answer. Use the following 5 point scale range of 1 to 5: (1 = Strongly Disagree, 2= Disagree, 3= Neutral, 4= Agree and 5 = Strongly Agree to)	Score
1. You maintain a good balance between your work endeavors, hobbies and home life.	
2. Your work motto would best be described as "working to live" versus "living to work".	
3. You find a balance of joy and fulfillment in your work goals when compared to goals at home.	
4. You use your yearly vacation/time off available to you from your employer.	
5. You get along well with everyone at your place of employment.	
6. You believe in giving your employer a hard day's worth of work.	
7. Your peers and supervisors view you as responsible and trustworthy.	
8. You are the "go to" person whenever anything important is needed.	
9. You tend to be the one to volunteer for special assignments or projects.	
10. In your work environment, people see you as a valued member of the team.	
Total Score	

Student, Volunteer, Unemployed or Retired

Complete the following survey by placing a score next to each question that best describes your answer. Use the following 5 point scale range of 1 to 5: (1 = Strongly Disagree, 2= Disagree, 3= Neutral, 4= Agree and 5 = Strongly Agree to)	Score
1. You maintain a good balance between your activities, hobbies and home life.	
2. Your motto would be best described as "working to live" versus "living to work".	
3. You find a balance of joy and fulfillment working with others.	
4. You use your available time to relax and recharge your personal battery.	
5. You attempt to get along well with everyone when working voluntarily in a team environment or activity.	
6. You believe in always giving 100% effort in your daily activities.	
7. You are viewed as responsible and trustworthy by your peers, friends, volunteers, etc.	
8. You are the "go to" person whenever anything important is needed when working with others.	
9. You tend to be the first to volunteer when working in teaming environments.	
10. When in a team environment, people see you as a valued member of the team.	
Total Score	

Community	Score
Complete the following survey by placing a score next to each question that best describes your answer. Use the following 5 point scale range of 1 to 5: (1 = Strongly Disagree, 2= Disagree, 3= Neutral, 4= Agree and 5 = Strongly Agree to)	
1. You are actively involved in your local community, church, social group, schools, etc.	
2. You are likely to volunteer for an event that would make a difference in your community.	
3. You are likely to offer neighbors help if you become aware assistance is required.	
4. You see it as your duty to give something back to your community.	
5. If a local disaster occurred, you would volunteer your help as needed.	
6. You attend local events (fairs, concerts, parade, etc.) to support the community in which you live.	
7. You know most, if not all neighbors on your block.	
8. You regularly frequent local store, restaurants, etc. to support the local business community.	
9. You share your skills sets (mind, body, voice) readily to help improve things in your community.	
10. You are aware of and get involved with the important issues that impact your local community.	
Total Score	

Now that you have completed all of the Xente assessments, take the total of each assessment and place them in the grid below Then total all assessments to see where you fall on the Xente Lifestyle Scorecard.

Xente Lifestyle Points Matrix
Insert assessment score In their corresponding section, then add for your total Xente Lifestle Score

Family	Vocation	Friends	Community	Self	Total

Note: Feel free to substitute any of the available assessments to fit your particular need or situation (Maximum of five assessments)

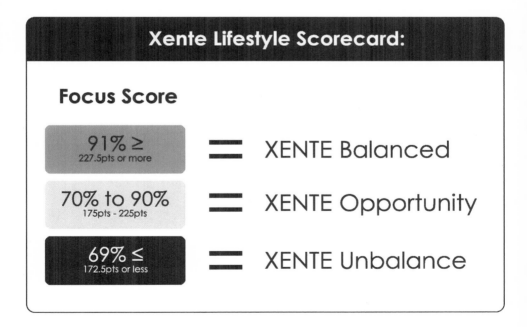

Xente Lifestyle Scorecard:

Focus Score

91% ≥
227.5pts or more
=== XENTE Balanced

70% to 90%
175pts - 225pts
=== XENTE Opportunity

69% ≤
172.5pts or less
=== XENTE Unbalance

Note: When you fall into the "Xente Balanced" level, you still need to continue to work at this to keep successes thriving.

19

Xente Lifestyle Examples

Now that you understand how the Xente Lifestyle Scorecard works, I want to provide you with some examples that may help you get started on your new journey of connecting with your complete life.

Essential Area Focus: Family

Whether you are married or a single parent, the kids seem to only get what's left over after you have done all of the "essentials" of your day, and sometimes that's done in a half-committed fashion.

Connect: Announce a family fun night (no television, no work, no cell phones, etc.). Mom and Dad (or a single parent) will be hosting. Go as far as letting the kids know that this event is all about them, and even ask them what would make this time an even more engaging experience for them.

Activate: Be very intentional about making this happen, parents. Do not get involved with any other activities, causing a delay of your connection goal. Make sure you follow through on this plan exactly as you stated you would.

Impact: Doing this lets your kids know that you really care about spending time with them. Caution: kids are very sensitive to promises made to them. They are very impressionable. Therefore, remember that they are still learning from you about commitment and especially about what is important to you.

Essential Area Focus: Significant Other

Connect: You both have been very busy, and making time for one another has been limited. Today you will commit to taking a short walk with one another after work before you engage in any other household or family business. This may require some coordination if you have younger children, but do make the arrangement.

Set the time and place to execute this commitment. This step is meant to be intentional, to help bring this essential area and others into focus. Remember, things just don't happen or come together randomly like when we were kids.

Activate: To gain success in this area, you have to be intentional about it. If you fail to plan, you can plan on failing. On that walk, remember that this is all about you two. We have to be able to separate your work life from your home life. During that walk, talk about something like the first time you met and how it made you feel. The topic can be about anything, as long as it involves you both sharing in the process.

Impact: This all may feel a bit rehearsed to you in the beginning because you will be very conscious of everything you are doing. It's okay! The idea is to establish a pattern of connectivity. The more you connect, the more natural each interaction becomes; and before you know it, you each will be excited about what ideas or plans are being made for the next connection (keep in mind that reciprocation is a vital part of connecting effectively).

Essential Area Focus: Community

Connect: This is one of the areas that can bring a great deal of joy and happiness, not only to others but to you as well. Most people are so preoccupied with their own lives that they do not even think of the true impact they can make in a church, community, or even with a next-door neighbor. Keeping this in mind, this week you will either reach out to your church (or any local institution of interest) or community organization to find out what you personally can do to give back. This can be as simple as volunteering at the local food bank or food pantry; giving just an hour of your time will make a world of difference. This can also be done with your spouse or significant other or (preferably) the entire family.

The idea here is that connecting in this way is truly selfless, and it allows you to explore meaning in connecting to a world outside of your immediate scope of responsibility. It will also let you see how small the world can be and how we are all connected in the scope of life.

It also establishes in your children an incredible foundation of charity toward mankind, whether they are directly involved or simply observing your commitment in this area.

Activate: You have confirmed that you and the family will participate in the food pantry this coming weekend. Sit with the family and discuss out loud why it is important to give back; prepare them for the event. Upon successful completion of the day's event, sit with the family and discuss what happened during that day and what the potential impact might be. Again, this will reinforce the idea of giving back, and it will also create another opportunity to perpetuate the family connection.

Impact: The entire family was able to be involved with giving something back to the community. Incredible memories and family bonds can be created when everyone is rallying around a greater cause for the good of others. When everyone has an opportunity to experience a feel-good moment as a family unit, it tends to be the most cherished memory.

Essential Area Focus: Vocation

Connect: This may seem to be a no-brainer to you, but it will require you to think and be creative. Oftentimes we can get very robotic about our jobs, and we rarely think about the importance of engagement. Keeping this in mind, you will go to work and do something totally unexpected to improve a relationship with someone you have been struggling with. Again, this does not have to be overly complex but should be meaningful enough that it will make a noticeable difference to the individual you are targeting. Today you will offer to take that coworker to lunch, so that you may get to know each other better.

Activate: You will send that individual a Xente connection request, inviting him or her to lunch. Keep in mind that your coworker's schedule may not allow him or her to connect on that specific day. But that's okay; move forward with the invite, extending another potential day that will be best for your coworker.

This will let your coworker know that your invitation wasn't a shot in the dark but one you are committed to making happen.

Impact: The one thing I have learned over my lifetime is that people rarely take the time to really get to know others. Because of this, we tend to misread or misdiagnose the true disposition of others. Taking the time to get to know others often reveals something you didn't know about the other person that gives you valuable insight or a reason to care more than you did before.

Essential Area Focus: Yourself

Connect: Now comes the opportunity to make it all about you. You can indulge in many different areas, whether it's exercise, your friends, reading a good book, engaging in one of your favorite hobbies, etc. This week, your connection will be your favorite hobby. It doesn't matter what activity you decide, as long as it is centered on connecting with yourself in some form or fashion.

Activate: You will send a Xente invite to three of your friends for a round of golf.

Upon completion of your outing, you will take some additional time to relax and think about some other specific ways of introducing connection ideas into your Xente lifestyle. This will help you plan for success versus aimlessly wondering about what's next.

Impact: One of the biggest challenges for individuals or married couples is the feeling of never getting time for yourselves. In the golf example, even though this person was not alone, he or she more than likely enjoyed the connection. It was time spent the way he or she wanted, which put that person in a better state of mind to focus on other areas of life, once the time was completed. Keep in mind that focusing on yourself as an essential area isn't always about how you get time alone.

Essential Area Focus: Extended Family, No Children

Connect: As life gets busy, this is the one area that always seems to take a back seat to everything else. For that reason, you want to break the cycle of absence and reach out to one of your family members, to rekindle your connection with him or her.

It has been almost nine months since you have seen your niece, Lisa. Lisa is your only niece, and she just started high school this year. You will make contact with your niece and propose a time that you two can spend some time together.

Activate: You arrange to pick up your niece in accordance with your agreement, and you head to the mall. There you pick up a couple of items for her, to celebrate her first year in high school, and you top that off with a nice lunch, during which you spend time catching up. During your time together, you make a pact that you will make an effort to stay in closer contact with one another. You invite her to connect on the Xentelife mobile apps on the Apple and Google stores.

Impact: You establish an important connection with an extended family member, giving you a stronger connection with your niece and creating an important value system in her, to show that family is important. This may begin an important tradition that could carry forward to another generation.

Essential Area Focus: Friends

Connect: Heading off to college can be an exciting but tough time for friends. You have been away at separate colleges since the start of the fall semester; it is now nearing the Christmas break. You have not seen your best friend since that time. You promised that no matter what, you would always remain best friends. Anticipating being home for the Christmas break, you want to reserve time in advance with your friend to go and hear your favorite band.

Activate: You go online and purchase tickets to see the band. Then you send your friend a Xente invite, letting her know that you have a couple of tickets to see your favorite band during the second week of your Christmas break at home.

Impact: You have shown a good friend how much you've missed her and established a selfless act that will most certainly be heartwarming to your friend.

As a result, your friend will want to show you her appreciation and think of a way to show her gratitude, perpetuating a great friendship filled with mutual sharing for years to come.

Reconnect (this applies to all of the prior connection examples shared): You should always take some time to reflect on the impact of each of your connections, asking what that connection was all about, how you might have done better, and if you simply went through the motions or really invested yourself into that connection. Answering these questions honestly will help you hone in on your next connection experience. It's not just about connecting; it's about being *intentional* about the connections you are making. It's through your sincere connection that you will begin to see the success in them. Once you have validated your results, think of your next connection as appropriate. Remember to pace yourself; it's perfectly okay to allow some time in between each of your connections, but ensure you keep the balance.

Because we are creatures of habit, we will have the tendency to slip back into our old habits. There are a couple of tools and anecdotes I want you to know about that are available to you through xentelife.com. The first is systemic. I have built prompting mechanisms into a specially designed mobile app for IOS and Android devices. The Xentelife mobile applications specifically designed to send you reminders based on your parameters to make meaningful connections by invitation to each of the relative essential areas of your life.

Systemic:

For instance, you may receive a platform generated message that will say something like "It's been a while since your last connection. Please make a Xente connection today."

Next you can retake all of the assessments via the Xente mobile applications, to determine where you are against the Xente Lifestyle Scorecard and begin where you need the most attention. Because we know the challenges you will face after reading this book; keep in mind the app was created to help support everything you learned in this book. So don't delay in downloading this resource today.

Helpful Suggestions:

Because our habits are like addictions, there are some very important points to consider prior to and during your journey of connecting. These suggestions, while passive in nature, should give you something to think about before you take on this lifestyle. They are:

- Make a plan and stick to it
- Keep your desired result in view
- Study your history of shortcomings and avoid them
- Set small goals, but execute then in a big way
- Be thankful for what you have; and know that success is only a connection away

20

Summary/Reflection

Friends, no matter what profile you fall into or what walk of life you come from, everyone has the opportunity to experience real success by making simple adjustments in what they intentionally decide to focus on.

The fact is, you are Xente because you get up every day, making an honest effort at living your life with the highest integrity and to the best of your ability, working with what your God gave you. You truly experience real success every day but have fallen into the trap of feeling there is only one type of success that matters, and that is absolutely not true.

The Xente lifestyle is completely realized when you not only embrace the fact that life is more than your vocation or the money you earn, it is your ability to find success in all aspects of your complete life and be intentional about who you connect with and how.

Join me today. Make a simple commitment to look at the six Xente essential areas of life and begin to appreciate the success you have made. Create new successes, bringing your life's journey to new heights. You are Xente. Embrace it!

A State of Reflection

As you are surely in a reflective state of mind after reviewing this book, I hope you are energized to the point of action. I also want to share that if we are being totally realistic, we cannot always completely change the human condition or fallout created when we pour ourselves into our dreams or desires to become successful. But what I can say with great confidence is that if we give the rest of the essential areas of our lives half as much attention as we give our vocation, we will find the kind of happiness that will begin to realign the things that matter the most.

This process of taking control of our lives in this way is a radical departure from the norm, and it will require us to take a step back and ask ourselves: what are we chasing, why are we chasing it, and is it worth sacrificing every other aspect of our lives to achieve it?

While working through this process, you may also want to ask yourself: have I been way too hard on myself or those around me? Only you can answer that, and those around you can certainly confirm it. If we are totally honest, most of us can answer the question without any help at all.

You are Xente once you realize that your honest efforts to be successful do not exclusively sit with having met your traditional success goal in life but with the realization that success is how you balance the multiple areas of your whole life. There are no limits to where you can take this simple process; you can make incredible strides that will begin to transform your life as long as you live.

In case you're wondering how this lifestyle approach helped me, I can say without pause that during the preparation, writing, and reading of this book, I radically increased my focus in the other essential areas of my life. It's peculiar, but intuitively I knew all along that my life was lacking the vital connections it needed to bring some semblance of balance and fulfillment. It was also peculiar that even when I was conscious of it, often it was very hard to change the things I had been doing out of habit.

They say you schedule the things that matter the most to you, so I took that premise and owned it. I became a student of scheduling and engaging the rest of my existence. During this time, I learned that while my vocation was and still is an important part of my life, easing off the work pedal a bit to divert some of that energy to other essential areas of my life actually made me more effective at work. (Who would have thought?)

As a result, I finally began to see the value of connecting and how it restored some of the broken areas of my life. I also began to notice how my loved ones responded by saying that Xente time was really making a positive difference in the quality of their lives. In fact, Xente time has become the holy grail of connections in my household, simply because it represents making a commitment to what really matters. The encouraging aspect of all of this is everyone understands it and has begun to incorporate it into their lives.

If by the slightest chance you are still wondering about the importance of connecting to what matters or need a reminder of how fragile or fleeting our existence can be, consider this. As I was working through the finishing touches of this book, I was presented with yet another reason to connect, activate, and reconnect (C.A.RE) even more to what truly matters. On July 29, 2016, my forty-five-year-old brother, Eric L. Johnson, a proud veteran of the

United States Marine Corps, passed away in his sleep of a heart attack. Even though I know the sting of his sudden death will stay with me for an extended period of time, I am extremely happy and proud that my brother and I were able to know and experience a deeper connection as a result of the writing and living of *The Success Makeover*.

My parting question to you once again is, "What will be the catalyst to help you engage your life and the people around you more completely?"

Xente: connect to what matters!

21

Xente Connection Invite

Please utilize our connection platform by downloading the Xentelife mobile applications from the Apple Store or Google Play Store to begin a new path to success and connect to what matters. If you do not have a means to connect online, please utilize the following table to help you track your connections. Simply add your desired essential element (Spouse, family, friend, vocation, community or self) to the "connection type" boxes on the next page to begin planning your next invite.

Xente Connection Invite | Sample

Connection Type	Spouse	Friends	Community	Vocation	Self
	✗				
Connection Date	6/6/2012				
Connection Goal	Go for a long walk to the Naperville River Walk				
Connection Results	Went for a walk to local ice cream parlor on the river and had great conversation about when we met.				
Key Learning's	I learned my wife feels alone most of the time and really appreciates when we can have simple time together.				
Next Connection Idea	Want to surprise my spouse and plan a picnic at the local arboretum where we visited as high school sweethearts.				

Xente Connection Invite | Sample

Connection Type					
Connection Date					
Connection Goal					
Connection Results					
Key Learning's					
Next Connection Idea					

Make connecting to what
matters easier.

Download the "Xentelife"
Mobile App today.

Visit our website or purchase
Xente gear at:

www.xentelife.com

About the Author

Kevin Johnson, married, two daughters, two grandchildren and currently living in a western suburb of Northern Illinois is a reformed workaholic executive in "Corporate America" who has dedicated nearly 25 years of his career working up the corporate ladder. His most notable experience among others include working for three major multi-national corporations serving in middle to upper level management roles over the course of his career. Having sacrificed countless moments over the years with those that mattered the most, Kevin confessed his greatest triumph came the day he finally accepted that true success in life was simply a function of how well he connected with all essential areas of his existence. These connections included intentional and genuine time with his spouse, family, friends, community, himself and yes his work. Visit him online at www.xentelife.com.